WE NEVER WANTED
A PARADE

Jim — you old
Devil Dog — hope
you enjoy this book
as much as I enjoyed
writing it! keep your
powder dry and your
head down!
    Semper Fi!

        Don

WE NEVER WANTED
A PARADE

DONALD G. TACKETT
SERGEANT, UNITED STATES MARINE CORPS
SERGEANT MAJOR, UNITED STATES ARMY, RETIRED

BOOKLOGIX®
Alpharetta, Georgia

ISBN: 978-0-615-72988-6

Library of Congress Control Number: 2012922444

Printed in the United States of America

♾This paper meets the requirements of ANSI/NISO Z39.48-1992 (Permanence of Paper)

The author has tried to recreate events, locations, and conversations from his/her memories of them. In some instances, in order to maintain their anonymity, the author has changed the names of individuals and places. He/she may also have changed some identifying characteristics and details such as physical attributes, occupations, and places of residence.

DEDICATION AND THANKS

This book is dedicated to all of the United States Marines that served with Kilo Company, Third Battalion, Seventh Marines, First Marine Division, Vietnam.

A special dedication goes to three of my squad members. They served faithfully and gave their lives for their country and their fellow Marines:

Lance Corporal Marvin Galbraith, KIA, 27 March 1968

Lance Corporal Richard Lopez, KIA, 27 March 1968

Lance Corporal Steve Davis, KIA, 24 April 1968

I would also like to dedicate this book to a special Marine, my squad leader for five months. This man saved my life and the lives our squad members on more than one occasion.

Corporal Frank Powers, WIA, 27 March 1968

One more special dedication goes to a young soldier that I did not know. I do, however, know his wife, Mrs. Eve Lamb Phillips, and she is one of the people who inspired me to write this book. Even after suffering the loss of her husband to the horrors of war in Afghanistan.

Corporal Matthew Phillips KIA, 13 July 2008

There are many people I would like to thank for encouraging me to write this book.

First, I would like to thank my wife, Sue and kids, Shannon and Bubba. They were the ones who had to put up with all my nonsense for all those years; the many deployments, missed birthdays, and holidays. They stood by me during my entire military career. They had to deal with my anger, my outbursts, and my temper. Although I don't show my emotions, I know they know I love them and without them this book would not have been possible.

I would also like to thank Mrs. Judy Austin. Judy asked me to talk to her Honors English class in 2008 about Vietnam. I had never really talked about my time in "The Nam" until then. After meeting with her and her class, I found a mental release that I had not ever felt before. Judy encouraged me to write my own book and took the time to edit it for me. I know it was quite the task for her because she took the time out of her busy work and home schedules to do this for me and to keep me on the right track. It was in her class that I met Mrs. Eve Lamb Phillips. Eve talked candidly about her husband's deployment to Afghanistan and how proud she was of him during lunch the day we met, only to lose her husband five months later in combat. I cannot say enough about these two fine educators.

I want to add one special person to the thank you list. His name is Staff Sergeant Tim Bellinger. Tim is my neighbor and a master Infantryman. He has been on active duty as well as a squad leader in the Georgia Army National Guard. Tim has deployed to both Iraq and Afghanistan as an Infantry squad leader. I have spent many evenings talking with Tim who has allowed me to vent about my horrors of war and I have also listened to him. We talked about things only warriors can understand and I am grateful he is my friend.

And last, but certainly not least on the thank you list are the Marines of Kilo Third of the Seventh, who have helped me remember many of the events I talk about in this book. My goal was to depict my stories as accurately as possible. Without their insight, I would have floundered with many of the events. My memory is not what it was many years ago.

It was my clear intent not to embarrass anyone or tell any story in this book without knowing the full circumstances of what happened. If I have offended anyone, I am truly sorry.

Thank you, everyone.

Semper Fi

Contents

PREFACE

I thought every day in the bush would be my last. I just knew today was the day I would get hit. Sir Charles definitely had his shit together in the Arizona Territory. When I turned every corner I could visualize confronting the little bastard that would end my life. It was a very scary thought. If that wasn't enough, we had to deal with the booby traps. The Arizona was littered with them. Then the night would come. It was so dark we couldn't see the guy next to us, let alone seeing out into the bush where we just knew a sapper was going to sneak up and cut our throats during the night. Then daybreak would come. Thank god for daybreak. We'd lived another day, another day closer to going home to the land of the big PX.

I unwrap myself from my poncho liner, used more to ward off the mosquitoes than to keep warm with. Slowly I could see movement from around the perimeter. I get up from my fighting position, quickly dug the night before, after a sapper attack on our position. My rifle is in my hand, it has become an extension of my body. A Marine goes nowhere without it. It becomes another appendage, and without it, we feel naked.

Over to my left is Mike R. Because of a shortage in squad members, seven total, Mike had to stay in his hole alone last night. He had to be scared. Mike was throwing something out of his hole. During the previous night's action, with the light of mortar illumination, I could see Mike digging frantically with his entrenching tool during the fight. I thought he was trying to make his hole deeper.

I watched in amazement as I figured out what Mike was tossing from his hole was a headless body of one of the sappers that attacked our position the night before. Mike had spent the entire night with the body in his hole. We didn't know it at the time, but Mike was in a desperate hand to hand fight for his life. Then he held up the sappers head by the hair as if to display a trophy and threw it down the hill. Mike left Viet Vietnam a week or two later. I saw him at a reunion in 2004. He was never the same. His wife told me of the horrors of nightmares along with several suicide attempts during their marriage. Mike did not remember that night.

Welcome home, Mike

In the hole to my right were Ricky Lopez and Mike S.

They went about the morning routine as if nothing had happened the night before. They were arguing about a c-ration pound cake that had mysteriously disappeared during the battle the previous evening. Of all things to worry about! Ricky would be killed in action a month and a half later on the night of 27 March 1968. All of a sudden pound cake didn't seem so important.

Welcome home, Ricky

My squad leader, Frank, was moving around the perimeter reissuing ammo, pyro, and more c-rations and giving everybody a warning order that we are about to move out. We are all waiting for the immortal words, "saddle up" Frank is a hero in his own rights, already receiving one Bronze Star with "V" device, and two Purple Hearts. He saved my life on more than one occasion. He would be seriously wounded and receive his third Purple Heart on the night Ricky and Marvin were killed, 27 March 1968. Frank would never be the same either.

Welcome Home, Frank

As we try to figure out where we are, most of us don't have a clue. Frank tells us we will be humping another ten clicks (10,000 meters) deeper into the jungle. We know we're somewhere in Viet Vietnam, but that's about all. We're pretty sure the officers know where we are and where we're going, or at least we hope so. After another day of struggling through the jungle in the heat and humidity, we will stop again and repeat the action of the night before. This time though, we will dig our holes a little deeper! We will do it all over again, unless we meet the enemy. Then things change very fast.

Together we were called "Third Herd," Third Squad, Third Platoon, Kilo Company, Third Battalion, Seventh Marine Regiment, First Marine Division, Viet Vietnam.

Welcome Home, Third Herd

INTRODUCTION

The title of my book, *We Never Wanted a Parade*, was born in 1985 while I was assigned to duties as a First Sergeant in Charley Company, First Battalion, Fourth Infantry, Third Infantry Division, in Germany. Our Battalion Commander, LTC Stephen T. Ripey, decided that his monthly Officer Development Program would include Vietnam veterans that would discuss lessons learned from our experiences while in Vietnam.

Keep in mind, there were very few Vietnam veterans left in the Army at that time. Only the members of senior leadership were Vietnam veterans, and most of us were Privates and young Lieutenants or Captains while in Vietnam. I was the only former Marine in the group, all the rest were in the Army while in Vietnam.

During the question and answer period, the officers began to ask questions about how we felt about the protesters and the fact we never received any welcome home ceremony. When it came my turn to speak, I told them about my homecoming and how horrible it was. I said, "Hell, we never wanted a parade, we just wanted someone to say thanks for serving." The idea stuck in the back of my brain for years to come. I decided then if I were ever to write a book, that would be a good title.

The book was originally supposed to be a compilation of stories of other Vietnam veterans' homecomings, including mine. As the years wore on, it became obvious I would never get that accomplished.

In 2008, my neighbor, a high school student at North Forsyth High School in Cumming, Georgia, came up to me and said they were studying about the Vietnam War. They were reading a book called, *The Things They Carried*. Her teacher was looking for a Vietnam veteran that had served in a combat assignment to talk to her class and give a face to the war. My neighbor asked if I would like to talk to her class. I at first said no. I really didn't like talking about the war, and definitely not to a bunch of high school kids. She continued to bug me for the next couple of days, so I called her teacher to see what she wanted me to do. I was still reluctant to do it, but said I would check it out anyway.

I was finally able to talk to Mrs. Judy Austin, my neighbor's teacher, who asked if I would be willing to talk to her Honors English class. She explained the kids were very excited at the opportunity to listen to me talk, especially after reading the book.

I finally said I would do it, and a date was set. I will be the first to admit that I was nervous as hell. I had to keep my language in check, which for me was very difficult to do. I always said I could stand up in front of a battalion of soldiers or Marines and not be nervous, but to talking to a bunch of high school kids was very nerve racking.

The day finally came when I was to speak. I went into the classroom between classes and met Mrs. Austin. She introduced me to another teacher, Mrs. Eve Lamb Phillips, who asked if it would be okay if she sat in the class and listened. I said of course it would be okay.

I talked to four or five of Mrs. Austin's honors classes that day. I will tell you, it was one of the most liberating experiences of my life. The kids asked very interesting questions. At the end of the classes, most of them came up to me and shook my hand, thanked me, and welcomed me home. What a shock. I have gone back every year now since 2008. In 2010, I was invited to speak to every senior class in the high school. The other teachers heard about the reaction and effect my stories had and thought it would be a good idea for me to speak to the entire senior class. Again, I was nervous as hell, but I did it. It was a great experience for me.

Talking about some of my experiences felt like a huge weight had been lifted from my shoulders. When I talked to Mrs. Austin about writing a book about other soldier's homecomings from Vietnam, she said that I should write a book about my own experiences. With her and Eve Phillip's encouragement, I began to write. Without the experience of talking to Mrs. Austin's class and the encouragement of those two outstanding educators, I probably would never have written anything. The result of their pushing me forward is, *We Never Wanted a Parade*.

CHAPTER 1

MY STORY, FROM THE BEGINNING

Some people spend an entire lifetime wondering if they made a difference, the Marines don't have that problem.

– Ronald Reagan

My story begins in 1967. I was about to graduate high school. I was amazed I was going to graduate at all. I had a sterling 1.8 grade point average. Band was my favorite subject, and my life seemed to revolve around playing the drums and my girlfriend. We had been dating for a long time. She was an A student and a majorette in the band. I thought I was in love. I knew I would not be going to college—I just wasn't interested. I also knew there was a good possibility that I would be drafted into the military. I knew my girlfriend would be going to college because she was smart and motivated. That caused me concern because I knew we would probably not be together much longer. But that was the farthest thing from my mind.

I did graduate in May 1967 and continued to work at Rinks Bargain City. Rinks was the Walmart of our time. I had been working there for three years through high school, and figured I would continue to work there until I figured out what I was going to do with my life. I liked working there; I had no responsibilities other than work and my girl. I still lived at home, much to the dismay of my soon-to-be-stepfather, who wanted me out of the house as soon as possible. He was a total asshole, even though I didn't see it at the time. My mind was on two things: girls and making money. Well okay, one girl.

In mid-June of 1967, I found out my older brother had enlisted in the Air Force. I never really got along with either of my brothers at the time. When our father died in 1963, we all sort of went our own way in our lives. We were teenagers and had our own friends, so we never really hung out together anyway. I always wondered why he had joined the Air Force, but didn't really care. I did find out later he was about to be drafted. About a week later, I was leaving for lunch at Rinks. I walked outside, and there was a VW van parked by the curb painted red and blue with a Marine Corps emblem on the side. The side door was open, and this Marine was sitting at a small table inside the van with a young man talking to him about the Marine Corps. I stopped and listened for a minute. I was intrigued by the fact this Marine was not painting a positive picture about life in the Marine Corps. I remember seeing a poster outside the van with this mean looking Marine Corps Drill Instructor pointing his finger and saying, "We don't promise you a rose garden," on it. I was thinking, *hell, that's no way to get someone to enlist!*

As I listened, he continued to talk about how tough the training was and how it was very likely that after basic training, you would end up in this country called Vietnam. I remember hearing a little about Vietnam but never really paid much attention to it. The other kid left and the Marine ask me to come in and sit down. He asked what my situation was, and I told him I had just graduated and didn't have a clue what I wanted to do. I also told him my brother had just enlisted in the Air Force. He began to tell me how the real challenge for someone like me was the Marine Corps. I was still seventeen years old at the time and didn't know if I could enlist or not. He told me my mom would have to sign for me, or I could wait until my eighteenth birthday which would be July 13, about a month away. I told him I would have to think about it and went on my way.

A couple of days later, I found myself in the Marine Corps recruiting office ready to become a man. The recruiter didn't promise me anything but the challenge of making me a Marine. I remember while in the Marine Corps, I was only given a choice two times of what I would like to do. This was the first. The recruiter asked me if I would like to attend basic training in San Diego, California, or Paris Island, South Carolina. I decided on San Diego because I had relatives in Los Angeles and figured they would let me off on weekends to go see them. Little did I know, that would not be the case, and he didn't tell me anything different.

The next step was to meet with my mother that evening at home so she could sign the papers sending me off to war. I had not told my mom before that evening of my intentions to enlist, so when we sat down to dinner that night, I informed her of my decision and that a Marine recruiter would be stopping by later so she could sign the papers. My soon-to-be-stepfather was a very happy person—my mother was not. She asked me to consider joining the Navy like my father or the Air Force like my brother, but not the Marine Corps. I told her my mind was made up. I think I did it more to show my older brother I was tougher than he was or to impress my girlfriend who, by the way, did not know of my decision either. Who knows the real reason? I, to this day, don't really know why.

About an hour later, the recruiter showed up in front of my house in the red and blue VW van with the Marine Corps emblem on the side and marched smartly to the front door. We watched him walk up the side walk, "standing tall, and looking good, ought to be in Hollywood!" (A little chant I would learn later.) I was about to become a "Hollywood Marine." My mother, being the ever proper lady, politely asked him in. We sat in the living room; she offered him coffee; he politely declined. We got down to business. My mother asked him to tell her what exactly it entailed to become a Marine. He went through the entire procedure of attending basic training, being assigned a military occupational specialty (MOS), going to the appropriate MOS assigned Advanced Individual Training, receiving the first assignment, and then coming home on your first leave. She asked of the chance of my going to Vietnam. He looked her straight in the eyes, and said it was not possible, but probable. Most Marines were being assigned to units throughout Vietnam. At that point, my mother started to waiver. I could see her tearing up, but she knew I would enlist anyway on my eighteenth birthday. She reluctantly signed the papers that sealed my fate. I would go to basic training on July 11, two days before my birthday. My soon-to-be-stepfather was ecstatic. My mother—not so pleased. I remember the recruiter thanking my mother for entrusting the Marine Corps with her youngest son and leaving.

The next step was to tell my girlfriend. We were going out that Friday night, so I decided that would be the time. As our date was concluding on the side door of her house, I decided that was the time. As I explained my decision, she didn't seem surprised. I was a little taken aback that she did not break down and start crying and beg me not to go. I was kind of relieved actually. We went inside and she proceeded to tell her mom and dad what I had done. They had always liked me, and her dad stood up and shook my hand, and her mother hugged me and wished me luck. Maybe it was a gesture that they were glad to get rid of me because they knew I wouldn't be college bound and that their daughter could find a nice college boy. Who knew? But they seemed sincere.

The rest of my time at home seemed to go very fast and in a blur. I quit my job at Rinks so I could spend most of my remaining time with my girlfriend and the rest of the friends I had grown up with. Most of them made fun of me for joining the Corps, told me what a fool I was, and that sort of jabbing. It was all good natured, and I took it as such. My mother married my soon-to-be-stepfather the day before I left for basic training. We said our good-byes at the church as she left for her honeymoon, which I found to be ridiculous at their age; I think she was thirty-nine at the time. I was to spend my last night with my girlfriend at home. Her father had put an eleven o'clock curfew on her. I think he might have worried I was going to try to do bad things to her on my last night of freedom. Little did he know! She went to the airport with me the next day. My aunt drove us. It was a quiet ride; not much was said. I would sneak a kiss and cop a feel when I could, knowing it would be the last for a very long time.

We said our good-byes, and I met up with my recruiter and two other recruits at the airport, all of us heading for

Marine Corps Recruit Depot, San Diego, California. None of us had ever been on an airplane before, so it was quite exciting. The recruiter put me in charge, which I found strange because at five foot eight inches tall and 125 pounds, I was the smallest of the group. What was I supposed to do? My first challenge as a Marine, OORAH!

CHAPTER 2

WELCOME TO THE CORPS, MAGGOT

Boot Camp Photo

The brave have always defined what the rest of us wish to be, but bravery is misunderstood. It is not the absence of fear, but the will to overcome it.

– Unknown Marine

RECEIVING BARRACKS

Our first plane ride was uneventful, except for one incident. My two fellow recruits didn't seem to be bothered by what was about to happen to us, but I was scared to death. Both were tough guys from the block: A white guy from a small town outside Columbus named Larry Six and a black guy from the inner city of Columbus named Bogey. We had about a two hour layover in Dallas. They decided to go to the bar and get a beer. I was seventeen and in charge, so I told them that was not a good idea; besides, I wasn't old enough to drink. I don't know how old they were, but they were definitely older and wiser to ways of the street than I was. They told me to fuck off and go where I wanted. Not wanting to show weakness, I joined them. While waiting at the bar, I became very nervous. The bartender walked over, and Larry ordered three draft beers. The bartender looked at us and laughed.

Bogey told him, "Look, we're headed to the Marine Corps, and we want a beer." The bartender laughed again, but served us the beer anyway.

I drank mine very slowly, not knowing the effects of alcohol at the time. I didn't want to show up drunk for basic training and make a bad impression on my drill instructor. Larry and Bogey continued to slam down drafts. When it was time to go, they were intoxicated to say the least. I shuttled them off to the plane, hoping they wouldn't cause a commotion and get us kicked out of the airport. Bogey was quite boisterous, and Larry wasn't quiet either, yelling something about becoming Marines. We got on the plane okay, and they both promptly fell asleep. It was already about eleven o'clock in the evening, and we all had a long day. We couldn't wait to get to our bunks and get a good night's sleep when we arrived so we could get a fresh start after breakfast in the morning. We figured out real quick upon arrival that was not going to happen.

The plane arrived sometime around one or two in the morning. I didn't know what to expect, where to go, or who was going to meet us. As we exited the plane, I noticed a very large Marine at the end of the terminal dressed just like our recruiter, standing with his hands on his hips and a very nasty look on his face. The one thing that stood out in my mind was his head gear. It resembled a "Smokey the Bear hat" and was formally called a campaign hat. The first thing I thought was, *don't call it a Smokey the Bear hat*. My recruiter did give me some words of wisdom before departing. As he told me, "Never speak unless spoken to." Advice that I would soon learn was invaluable.

As we walked closer to him, he started yelling right in the middle of the terminal at us. He said, and I will never, ever, forget this, "Maggots, you better get your asses on the double time."

I didn't know what double time meant, but I assumed it meant we better start running. I had three folders with my team's orders in them because I was in charge, so I told Larry and Bogey we better get moving.

Larry started to move, but Bogey said, "I ain't running for nobody. I'm taking my fucking time." I was flabbergasted. I told him to move it, he told me to go to hell, or some other terms not so nice, followed by, "you honky."

When we got to the drill instructor, he saw I had the folders, so he yelled, "Are you in charge of these maggots?"

I replied, "Yeah." My first mistake in the Marine Corps.

He immediately got in my face screaming at the top of his lungs that the first and last thing out of my filthy sewer mouth would be "Sir."

I yelled as loud as I could, "Sir, yes sir."

He grabbed the envelopes from my hand and asked me, since I was in charge, why the hell wasn't I kicking the shit out of the other maggot that would not double time. I learned right then and there that there was never a correct answer for the drill instructor. As Larry and I got down in the front leaning rest position (push up position) right there in the middle of the airport, with people getting off planes staring at us, Bogey was still some thirty feet away, taking his time. The drill instructor put his attention on him. Bogey was taken outside to two other waiting drill instructors. We never saw him again. The drill instructor came back in, got us, and directed us to go outside and join the other group of maggots waiting for the bus.

What a shock. I had only been in the Marine Corps ten minutes, and I was already a maggot, I had a filthy sewer mouth, and nobody liked me. *Oh my god, what in the hell did I get myself into?*

The bus ride to the base from the airport was nothing but a series of yells, fear, curses, and smacks in the back of the head. We had to sit at attention, looking straight ahead, with our hands on our legs just above our knees, fingers extended and joined (Don't know why, but it was very important to keep your fingers extended and joined). Upon arrival, we had exactly ten seconds to "un-ass" his Marine Corps bus. It was assholes and elbows as everyone struggled to not be the last one off. We learned very quickly that being the last one to do anything was not a good place to be. We were directed to sets of yellow footprints painted on the pavement in front of the receiving barracks. The footprints were painted so our feet would be in the perfect position of attention (forty-five degree angle), a position we stayed in most of the time during basic. As we continued to be berated, yelled at, spit on, and chewed out, we were told to look up and read the sign just above the entrance of the receiving barracks, it was the Recruits Creed, I read:

TO BE A MARINE

YOU HAVE TO BELIEVE IN YOURSELF

YOUR FELLOW MARINES

YOUR CORPS

YOUR COUNTRY

YOUR GOD

SEMPER FIDELIS

We would find out later that the Recruit Creed would mean more to us than any of us would ever believe. The only thing that was missing was the part about your country believing in you. We believed in our country, but our country forgot to believe in us.

My uncle was a barber in Oklahoma, so when we were shuffled into the barber shop at three o'clock in the morning, I pictured my uncle standing there. Not to be. It was the fastest haircut I had ever had. We were told, if you have a mole on our head, to put your finger on it and state very loudly to the barber, "Sir, mole, sir." That way the barber would avoid cutting it off. I have a mole. I took the appropriate action, at which time the barber told me to move my fucking finger and promptly cut the mole off with all the rest of my hair. I left the barber shop, my head bleeding profusely. The drill instructor pulled me out of line and chewed me up one side and down the other for attempting to commit suicide my first day of basic training. No first aid was applied, I just continued to bleed. We found out later we were in what was called "zero week." Hell, our training would not even begin for another week or two— another week in hell.

For the next two hours or so, we continued through a long line of processing into the Corps. We were stripped of any civilian identity. The only jewelry allowed was a wedding ring. They told us to put everything we had in a box that would be mailed home, including our watches. They told us they would be telling us what time it was, so we didn't need one. As our life in the Corps continued, we found out they were right. We never knew what time it was, nor did it matter. Everything we did was by the numbers to an exact tee, teaching us attention to detail. We thought at the time it was just harassment; we would learn later attention to detail was essential to survive in combat.

By the time we hit the rack (bed), it was about 0400 hours. (You see, I'm starting to use military time now since I am a Marine, even if I'm a maggot Marine). Everyone was in shock, but passed out immediately. We thought we would get to sleep for a while—boy, were we wrong.

Exactly at 0500 hours, we were awakened by the drill instructor beating on the side of a garbage can, yelling at the top of his lungs, "Hit the road!"

Again, not knowing what he wanted, we all kind of looked at each other. He then started throwing us out of the building, so we understood that meant go to formation. Boy, did I have a lot to learn.

The days started to run together, and we did not know whether we were coming or going. We were issued ill-fitting uniforms that fit like potatoes sacks, we were not allowed to tuck in our shirts, or trim our belts to fit, or blouse our boots. Our covers (hats) were so big they fell down over our ears, giving the appearance of having floppy ears. We made Gomer Pyle look like a recruiting poster Marine. After being issued all of this equipment, which was foreign to all of us, we were headed to medical clearance. We were given extensive physical exams, dental exams, and many, many shots. The shots were given from a shot gun. Not the one we used to hunt squirrels with, but an air powered gun that forced whatever shot we took into our arms. We had to walk through a gauntlet of navy corpsmen, one on each side of us while we walked the line nailing us with the gun. The corpsmen seemed to really enjoy this. The only shot not in the arm was the famed Gamma Globulin shot. They gave it to us in the butt, and it left a softball size lump in our asses that was very difficult to sit on. Oh, the pain!

PLATOON ASSIGNMENT

We were finally through with zero week and were about to be assigned to a platoon to start week one. It seemed like we had already been there a month by that time, but in reality, has only been five days. We were called out by name and told where to stand. At the end, we had about sixty recruits in our platoon. It was Platoon 3028. We were told the senior drill instructor for our platoon was the meanest son of a bitch in all of Marine Corps Recruit Depot, San Diego. I'm sure they told all the platoons that, but we didn't know and could only take them at their word. All I know is we were scared.

About thirty minutes later, out walked two of the meanest looking DI's I had ever imagined. Staff Sergeant Shields was a mountain of a man. All of six foot five inches tall and broad at the chest and narrow in the waist. His arms looked like telephone poles. He was the assistant drill instructor (ADI). Our senior drill instructor was Gunnery Sergeant Monroe. He looked like a bull dog. He had the scariest, meanest look on his face that I had ever seen. His face never changed expression for the next eight miserable weeks.

I figured the way to get by was not to be noticed. I was in the third of four squads, near the end of the formation. There were a lot of bigger guys in front of me, so I figured I was safe. The senior drill instructor (SDI) started focusing on the biggest guys in the platoon. He began with a huge black man named Mackey. He made Mackey the first squad leader. Then he began picking the other squad leaders by their size also. I did not want to be a squad leader because they were always being called to the duty hut—another place we never wanted to be called to. During my first week in basic training, I was hardly noticed. I kept my stuff together, was never out of line and stayed in the background as much as possible. I endured the mass punishments dished out by the drill instructors and sucked it up. I figured if the next seven weeks went this well, I would be good to go. The SDI didn't even know my name, and that was good.

The SDI and ADI would put most of their attention on the people with a weakness. The two recruits that bore the brunt of most of their attention were recruit Herman Book and recruit James Fuchs. Book was very tall, lanky, and could not pronounce his R's. He kind of sounded like Elmer Fudd. So when the SDI would say something, instead of his answer being, "Sir, yes sir," it would sound like, "Su, yes su." Book was humiliated throughout basic training by the SDI and ADI.

Recruit Fuchs on the other hand was overweight. The fear of all recruits was that if we failed any part of the physical training portion of basic, fell out of runs, or were just plain unmotivated, we would be sent to what was called the "Physical Conditioning Platoon, or PCP." The SDI called it the "Pig Farm." Once you lost weight, became physically fit, or got your motivation back, you would then be recycled back to the beginning of basic training. This was a fear we had all the way through week eight. Nobody wanted to repeat basic. Fuchs was constantly harassed because of his weight. The SDI called him every name in the book, especially "fat, horrible, warthog." We encouraged Fuchs to do his best, and he did. He passed all the physical requirements, stayed motivated even in the continued face of constant humiliation and ridicule, and never fell out of a run. Fuchs graduated with our platoon. He was a proud Marine. PVT Fuchs was killed in action on 2 February 1968. He had only been in Vietnam for one month. He died a hero.

Welcome home, PVT Fuchs.

CHAPTER 3

PLATOON 3028: HONOR PLATOON

The Marines I have seen around the world have the cleanest bodies, the filthiest minds, the highest morale, and the lowest morals of any group of animals I have ever seen. Thank God for the United States Marine Corps.

– Eleanor Roosevelt

One of the first things Gunnery Sergeant Monroe explained to us was that he always won the honor platoon in the series. There were four platoons to a series. He had never lost, and was not about to lose this time. He had won all the skills streamers for the guide on, all eight. Nobody could match his ability to train and motivate recruits like he and Staff Sergeant Shields could. He said we were the worst of all his previous platoons and he planned on making us learn his way. We did not want to disappoint him, only because we were more scared of him then not. The first skills streamer would be handed out in three weeks; it was for close order drill (marching).

You've heard the expression, Cleanliness is next to godliness? Well, in platoon 3028, cleanliness was next to "senior drill instructor-ness." I know, that's not a word, but believe me, it was. He inspected every inch of our bodies after coming out of the shower, the squad bay, even the dirty laundry better be clean and folded in the laundry bags. He missed nothing. If we chewed our fingernails, he would know. While coming out of the shower room, he would stop each recruit and pull back the ear and check the nails for proper cleanliness and cut. He held a piece of metal, it was actually a piece of M14 rifle cleaning rod about six or eight inches long, and if he found dirt behind our ear, he would whack us on the ear with the rod. If we chewed our fingernails, he would whack us on the finger. It hurt like hell. I know, I was whacked more than once. I had chewed my nails my entire life. I stopped for eight weeks. When I graduated basic training, while on my way to our next training cycle, I chewed my fingernails until they bled.

Our living area was a Quonset hut, a metal building half-moon shaped, big enough for a squad of fifteen to sixteen recruits. It had bunk beds equally lined up on each side of the building. Each of us had one foot locker and one small wall locker to store our gear. Everything had its place; socks and skivvies (underwear) were folded and rolled with an exact science. Everything in the wall locker was hung with equal distance between each hanger and in proper order. The shaving kit had to be perfectly placed, and there had better not even be so much as a pubic hair on your soap. He checked everything, and when we thought we were good to go, he would find something else and tear up the entire area and make us start all over again.

There was a routine on how to get in the rack each night. We would be given commands. And we had to stand by our bunks at the position of attention. He would give the command, "Prepare to mount," pause for a second, then command, "Mount." We would lie at the position of attention. He would command, "Ready, pray," and we would say a quick little prayer or mumble something. He would then give the order to sleep, at which time we shut our eyes. Sleep wasn't hard to come by. We were pushed so hard during the day, we almost immediately fell asleep.

THE PARADE GRINDER

The parade grinder was nothing more than a huge flat concrete area where everyone learned to march. We spent most of the first three weeks on the grinder because of the upcoming close order drill competition. Imagine ten acres of concrete, in the middle of summer in San Diego. We could see the heat rising from the surface. The bad part was when we messed-up, we were put in the push-up position. The concrete was extremely hot, so that was motivation enough to do well. Of course, nothing was good enough for Gunnery Sergeant Monroe. Drill and ceremonies, and rifle marksmanship were his thing. He let us know from the beginning that he had never lost the series competitions in these two events and we had better not be the first platoon of his to lose. We knew the consequences. We would march all day long, with the exception of when we ate. Everyone had blisters on their feet. Nobody was used to wearing the boots we were issued, so our feet were a mess. Nobody complained or went on sick call; we just sucked it up. Nobody wanted to be recycled.

One of the worst recruits in marching was a man I'll call Rose. He had no timing, no rhythm, no coordination, nothing. He became the target of the SDI, which took the pressure off the rest of us. Like I said in the beginning, everything we did was done to an exact science and precise time. They controlled every aspect of our lives: when we ate, when we slept, when we trained, even when we went to the head (bathroom). We couldn't just raise our hands and ask to go pee. We did it at the same time as everyone else, or we waited. It was teaching us self-control. When we were on the parade grinder, Gunny Monroe would march us over to the head. We would go in a squad at a time. We better take care of whatever business we had, in a very fast manner, whether we had to or not. One day the SDI was working us very hard; it was hot; we had been on the parade grinder for it seemed like hours. He hadn't given us a head break in a long time.

All of a sudden, I heard a commotion in the formation. Recruit Rose had done it again. He couldn't hold it and peed all the way down the front of his uniform. The SDI went into a rage. He berated, punched, and slapped Rose several times for being a disgusting maggot. He then marched the entire platoon over to where the headquarters building was. He took Rose and made him stand at the position of attention in front of Headquarters as we marched off. I felt so sorry for Rose and I didn't know what to do. Of course, we couldn't do anything.

Awhile later, a sergeant walked up to our platoon while we were marching. The SDI halted the platoon and began an argument with the sergeant. The SDI was told to report to the Headquarters building. As we marched over, I noticed Rose was not in front of the building. We halted, stayed at the position of attention in front of Headquarters while the SDI went in. The sergeant remained with us. He put us at ease and asked us when the last time we drank water or used the head was. Everyone was afraid to speak, so nobody answered. He seemed to be compassionate and assured us nothing would happen if somebody answered. Finally the platoon guide said, "Sir, about two hours ago, sir." The sergeant replied that we did not have to call him sir; he was not a drill instructor. He then marched us to the head where we got our first and only break for the day. He put us in the shade while we waited for our SDI to come back and told us to relax, smoke, and drink water. Again, all of us were scared to death, but he assured us it was okay. Awhile later, we saw the SDI coming out of the Headquarters building. We immediately reacted getting back into formation without being told to do so. The SDI came up and again started berating the sergeant for taking us to the shade. They argued a little bit, names were called, and the sergeant went on his way. We never saw recruit Rose again.

We heard later on that the commandant of recruit training came out of the building and saw Rose standing there. He came up to Rose, saw that he had wet himself, took him in the building, and sent the sergeant to find our platoon. We were told the SDI was reprimanded and Rose was recycled to another platoon. It could not have been good for Rose because the drill instructors have their own little connections, and I'm sure Rose did not have it any easier in his new platoon, probably harder.

THE BROWN STATION WAGON

The SDI did not let up on us. The closer we got to the drill competition, the worse he got. We had become accustomed to his rants and raves, but we were doing better, or so we thought. We were on the parade grinder more and more. About a week before drill competition, we started seeing this old brown station wagon come up through the parking lot. The SDI would march us over to where the car was parked, put our backs to the car and put us at the position of parade rest, a modified position of attention. A huge argument would ensue. We figured out real quick that the individual in the brown station wagon was his wife. They would argue and cuss at each other for a while, and then she would leave. He would return to the platoon madder than when he left. All hell would break loose for us for the rest of the day. I could not imagine living a life where every time I saw my wife, there was an argument—and in earshot of everyone, too. I always hoped they didn't have any children, but didn't know, or dare to ask.

It seemed like every day, sometimes twice a day, we would see that horrible brown station wagon coming through the parking lot. We knew our day was just going to be a living hell. I think somebody must have complained because a day or two before the drill competition, the brown station wagon never returned. Maybe she had enough, maybe he had enough—we didn't know, and we didn't care. It was just a relief.

DRILL COMPETITION

The day of drill competition had finally arrived. We went through our normal morning routine like always. The SDI wasn't there that morning, which was strange because he was always there. Our ADI, SSG Shields was with us that morning alone. We knew the routine by now and could do it in our sleep. We had our uniform and weapons inspection by SSG Shields and marched to the parade grinder. We were thinking that maybe they got rid of the sadistic Gunnery Sergeant Monroe, and our spirits were lifted, only to have them dashed. When we arrived at the parade grinder, there he was and looking meaner than ever. He came over to us and told SSG Shields he would take it from there. Even though we were the first platoon in our series, he informed us we would be the last to march. He preferred we watch the other platoons perform so we could make mental notes of their mistakes and not make the same ones since the prescribed routine was the same for all platoons.

We watched the others perform what seemed to be flawless movements. We were scared. These guys were good, and obviously had put as much time into it as we had. My only thought was, *How in the hell are we going to beat these other three platoons?* Our time finally arrived. We marched out in front of the crowd. Six drill instructors we had never seen before were waiting with clip boards. They would be watching every step of the routine with eyes like eagles. They would miss nothing. We performed our routine with the expertise of a well-oiled machine.

We waited what seemed like an eternity for the results. The entire series was marched out onto the parade grinder in series formation, with our platoon all the way to the left. Several speeches were made by our series commander, a major, and our series first sergeant (who we had never seen before today) on how much progress we had made in just three weeks and how proud they were of all of us.

These were the first encouraging words we had heard since arriving here. They said it was a very close competition with the platoons only points apart. The winner was announced, it was Platoon 3028, our platoon. The series commander and first sergeant came up in front of our platoon, congratulated Gunnery Sergeant Monroe and pinned the marching competition streamer on our guidon. We were proud as peacocks. We hoped that would make the SDI happy, but again, that was not to be. When we arrived back at our platoon area, he began his rant on how horrible we had done, there was nothing to be proud of, and we were the worst platoon he had ever had. The purpose for his rant was that we had won the competition by only a few points, and that was not good enough for him. He left for the rest of the day, and we were left wondering what we would have to do to make this man proud of us.

The next week ended with our officially being half way through basic training. We started feeling and looking like Marines. We were allowed to starch our covers, which made them fit better. We cut our belts to fit and for the first time were allowed to blouse our trousers with blousing rubber bands. This signified we were almost good enough to be called Marines. Training continued, and we won two more streamers for our guidon. Three down, five to go, with the most important coming up: rifle marksmanship.

EIDSON RANGE, RIFLE MARKSMANSHIP TRAINING

It was finally time to find out if we could shoot; the trademark of a real Marine. We had been issued the M14, the best weapon in the Marine Corps inventory. The M16 was not in inventory at the time. We had been chanting a little chant in the barracks at night led by the SDI that was:

THIS IS MY RIFLE, THIS IS MY GUN, THIS IS FOR FIGHTING, THIS IS FOR FUN.

The whole meaning behind the chant was, the rifle was the most important piece of equipment we would ever be issued, and the gun was our penis. The two were not to be confused. So while doing the chant, our rifle would be held at right shoulder arms, and the left hand would be holding the penis. That way we would never, ever call a rifle a gun, even though that's what it is. The Marines also have many quotes about their rifles. You have probably heard them, especially in the movie, *Full Metal Jacket* (the most accurate portrayal of Marine Corps basic training I have ever seen). Two of the best quotes are:

THE DEADLIEST WEAPON IN THE WORLD IS A MARINE AND HIS RIFLE.

And of course, the ever popular

THIS IS MY RIFLE. THERE ARE MANY LIKE IT, BUT THIS ONE IS MINE. MY RIFLE IS MY BEST FRIEND. IT IS MY LIFE.

That quote continues on, but you get my point. To be a Marine, you had to be able to shoot. I had only held shot guns before entering basic, and that experience was limited to hunting squirrels with my dad and grandpa. And by the way, I never shot a squirrel either. Training was more relaxed at Eidson Range. We moved into new barracks with the entire platoon on one floor, open barracks with huge heads, with showers, much nicer than what we had become used to. Rifle training would last for two weeks. The first week was spent with what was called, "snapping in." These were days spent learning the different firing positions, aiming techniques, and trigger control. I remember one of the first acronyms I learned was:

"BRASS"

B – BREATH

R – RELAX

A – AIM

S – SLACK

S – SHOOT

I had taken to shooting like I was born to do it. Our daily punishments did not end, but seemed to be lighter. He wanted us to concentrate solely on shooting. Our SDI said he *never* had a recruit not qualify on the range.

The second day at Eidson Range, our squad leader, recruit Mackey, was relieved of his duties. He had dropped his rifle, a major sin, bending the sights. The SDI went into spasms with him. The SDI then did the unthinkable. He called me by name out of formation and told me I was now the first squad leader. I was terrified. So far, I had avoided his rants by staying in the background and not getting any unwanted individual attention. That he even knew my name was a surprise to me. I was now in charge of fourteen other recruits. I was responsible for not only I, but everything my squad did, right or wrong. Good god, I was one of the smallest ones in the squad; how could he do this to me?

The first week ended up with little to no attention paid to our squad. We seemed to be sailing through rifle marksmanship training.

Week two consisted of the real deal, shooting. This is where the rubber met the road. The first day we shot set the stage for how well we were treated—or not treated. All the SDI wanted for us to do was hit the target. Everyone in my squad hit the target except one recruit. The SDI took us both in his office that night and beat the hell out of us punches to the stomach and kidneys. Not hard, but enough to get our attention. He seemed to be getting more sadistic every week. Slaps to the head were a common occurrence, also, but that didn't bother me as much as the kidney punch. Day two, everyone did better with all of us hitting the target. We avoided punishment that night—except this time the barracks weren't clean enough, so we all did pushups, sit ups, side straddle hops, mountain climbers, and any other exercise he could think of until we puked. By the way, we had graduated from being called maggots to now being called pukes. We were moving up in the world.

The last two days were qualification days. If we failed to qualify the first day, we were given a second chance the next day. If we failed to qualify that day, we were recycled back two weeks in training. At that point, I expected to qualify as expert. I had been one of the platoon's top shooters all week and avoided the harsh punishments of the SDI at night. On day one of qualification, my entire squad qualified. I, however, missed qualifying expert by one point. I was disappointed beyond belief and felt the brunt of the SDI's displeasure with me that night. I spent the night in the broom closet with about ten other recruits who had disappointed him. He would, at different times during the night, take us one by one out of the broom closet to the head and perform different acts of punishment on each of us.

I know what most of you are thinking at this point is: Why didn't you fight back? Two reasons: the first was SSG Shields was as big as a mountain, and even though he never once touched a recruit, he was always there and always had Gunnery Sergeant Monroe's back. The fact was, we were too damned scared. The second reason was, we kept our eye on the prize, graduating and becoming Marines, and if that was what it took, then, so be it.

The last day of qualification was finally there. We had three recruits have to go back on day two because they failed to qualify on day one. Thank God, none were from my squad. We were lucky. Other platoons in the series had up to ten to fifteen recruits there on the second day. We spent most of the day preparing to return to our old barracks. When the recruits returned, they had all qualified, but it still wasn't over. The series commander would announce the winner of the marksmanship streamer after chow that evening. Everyone was on edge, especially the

SDI. He had never lost the streamer. We were afraid we would all be killed if we lost. That evening, the series held a formation to announce the winner. The series commander announced that platoon 3028 had won. We had a 100 percent qualification rate, and the most qualified experts in the series. When the series commander and first sergeant came in front of the platoon and pinned the Marksmanship streamer on the guidon, I thought I almost saw the SDI crack a smile. Four streamers down, four to go.

COMPLETION OF TRAINING

For the next three weeks, we saw less and less of the SDI. We had SSG Shields most of the time and a new drill instructor named SGT Shaw. He was new at being a drill instructor and spent more time training us than belittling us. We won two more series streamers, with only two left, barracks and equipment inspection, and the final and most important one, the commandant's inspection. This inspection would determine who would win Honor Platoon. Just because you won a lot of streamers didn't mean you would win Honor Platoon—that was decided by the commandant.

Training was almost over, and we felt more and more like Marines. Our dress uniforms were fitted and dry cleaned, and our utility uniforms were pressed and starched. All was good, for the time being.

The last week of training saw the worst thing that happened to me. We were at what was called drown proofing—a technique we learned on how to stay afloat in the water by using our uniforms to make a flotation device (and it does not include treading water). I took to drown proofing very well. This was all day training in the pool, so we were loving it. To qualify, we had to drown proof for thirty minutes without treading water. No problem for me, I was very comfortable in the water. Everything started out great. I was doing the exercise without a problem. The instructor announced the time as each five minutes passed. The last time he called out was twenty-five minutes, only five minutes remaining. Hell, I was doing great. I could have stayed there all day. I was relaxed, enjoying the view, but apparently got too close to the diving board. I heard the instructor yelling for me to move away from the diving board, so I slowly paddled away into the middle of the pool. He started yelling that I was treading water and jumped off the diving board right on top of me, dragging me to the bottom of the pool. Fear overcame me, but he held me under. I was drowning. I remember a calm coming over me as I looked up at the light from the sun reflecting on the water. I remember touching the bottom of the pool before I passed out. I had officially drowned.

I woke up lying on my stomach with the lower half of my body still in the water. The instructor had his foot on my back pushing down, pumping the water out of my body. I remember spitting up water and looking at my hands They were a weird color of blue. As I regained my senses, I noticed about ten or twelve recruits standing against the wall, the same color blue as me.

I heard the instructor yell, "he's ok," as he grabbed me by the arm, pulling me up out of the water and told me to report to the wall with the rest of the blue boys.

Blue boys, what? Anyway, we were all informed we had failed drown proofing and would have to repeat the training after noon chow. I was disappointed to say the least.

After lunch, we returned to the pool. I was devastated that I would have to do it again. It wasn't that I was incapable of doing it—it was because I had never failed to accomplish anything in basic training that I had started out to do. Of course, the SDI wasn't happy that one of his squad leaders failed either, so I felt the wrath of his anger after lunch. When we got back in the pool, there was the same blond haired instructor that had drowned me standing on the diving board, looking straight at me grinning with an evil grin. I knew he was going to try to drown me again, but this time I was ready and swore that if he grabbed me, I would hold onto him for dear life, and he would go down with me. As luck would have it, I stayed away from the diving board, completed the task with ease. I swore that if I ever saw that guy again, I would kick his ass as best as I could. I passed and awaited graduation.

Two days before graduation, we were in formation receiving the daily ass-chewing from the SDI when he announced he was allowed to promote six of us to private first class, E-2. He said since we were the worst platoon he had ever had, he didn't want to promote any of us, but the series commander told him he had to. I didn't have a clue, but I was one of the ones selected. I was to graduate with one stripe on my sleeve. No small feat since there were about sixty of us in our platoon. I was as proud as I could be when I turned my shirt in to have the one single mosquito wing stripe sewn on.

The night before graduation, he announced what our military occupational specialties would be and where we would go for further training the day after graduation. This was the moment we had all waited for. I had excelled in clerical and electronic skills in the tests we took prior to entering, so expected a job as a clerk or communications guy. Much to my surprise, he announced I was a 0311, light weapons infantryman. Go figure.

Graduation day was upon us, now we were all standing tall, looking good—ought to be in Hollywood. The SDI informed us that after graduation there would be no congratulations from him because we broke his winning streak. We did win Honor Platoon for the series, but we only won seven of the eight streamers. We lost the barracks and equipment inspection streamer. He hated us.

We graduated with the last words he said to us before dismissal. I will always remember what he said, "If I ever see any of you pukes in Vietnam, I will remember you, and I will kill you."

We knew he meant every word of what he said.

We congratulated ourselves as we went our separate ways, and we never saw Gunnery Sergeant Monroe again.

Platoon Commander
G/ Sgt. M.D. Monroe

Drill Instructor
S/ Sgt. L.M. Shields

G/ Sgt. Monroe and Platoon Guide
at Graduation

Pvt. Donald G. Tackett at Graduation

Pvt. Donald G. Tackett at Rifle Range

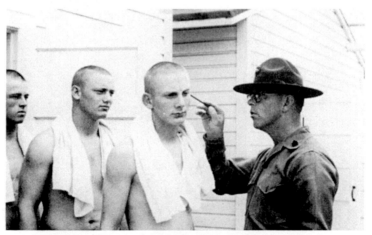

SDI Inspecting recruits cleanliness with his cleaning
rod so he didn't have to touch us with his hands

Sept. 1967

DONALD G. TACKETT

Pvt. Donald G. Tackett, son of Mrs. Frank Ferry of 1022 Sunset avenue graduated recently after completing eight weeks of recruit training at the Marine Corps Recruit Depot at San Diego, Calif.

He will undergo additional training in individual combat and be given a leave at home before reporting for his first Marine assignment.

Pvt. Donald G. Tackett Hometown News Release
September 1967

CHAPTER 4
THE MAKING OF A
UNITED STATES MARINE

Pvt. Donald Tackett
ITR
Camp Pendleton, CA

There are two kinds of people that understand Marines: Marines, and the enemy. Everyone else has a second opinion.

– General William Thornson

Although you might say the making of a United States Marine began in basic training, I tend to disagree. In basic, we were maggots, pukes, fat horrible warthogs, ladies, pissants, or any name—other than a United States Marine. I get it, I really do, but once I graduated, I felt like I was a Marine for the very first time. When we watched other recruits beginning their life in the Corps, we almost felt sorry for them.

We would say things like, "God they must be in week two or three. Boy, am I glad I'm not them."

We were given a four hour pass after graduation, at which time we were to meet up at a location where transportation would be taking us to our next destination. My destination and all other 0300 series Marines, infantry (notice I'm using the term Marines now, not recruits), were headed to Camp Pendleton, California for ITR, or Infantry Training Regiment.

For our first four hour on post liberty, most of us headed straight to the bowling alley for the first taste of cheeseburger, coca cola, and greasy french fries we had since enlisting. A lot of the others going to different locations in the United States had already left for the airport, and since Camp Pendleton was right up the road, we got liberty and a bus. We stuffed ourselves with every available bit of pogey bait we could get our hands on. Some guys drank beer, I did not. We left three hours later, sick as dogs. Our stomachs were not used to the abuse we had just put them through. Guys were throwing up all the way back to our formation area. I didn't throw up, but I sure wanted to. Besides, being one of the only ones with a stripe on my sleeve, I figured I had better try to set an example.

I had made friends during basic with several guys in our platoon. We hung out together while on liberty. We decided we would go to the formation area about thirty minutes early and rest up before we departed. We got there, and we met a stocky, mean-looking corporal waiting to escort us to Camp Pendleton. Come to find out he wasn't mean at all. He had just returned from Vietnam and was assigned to ITR, where we were going. Of course, we were full of questions for him about Vietnam, but he didn't seem interested. He was an Infantryman with Fifth Marines and was wounded twice. He was just biding his time until his discharge. He had about six months left in the Marine Corps. He was a very personable guy and tried to tell us what to expect in ITR. He would be in charge of us for our entire time in ITR, which, we found out, would be four weeks. It would be filled with small unit tactics, weapons training on all different types of weapons, escape and evasion, and lots of road marches. He said we would road march where ever we went, no trucks or buses, just boots on the ground. We found out during training that he was one tough little dude. He could road march us to death, he would just put his head down and go.

ITR

The buses arrived; we loaded up and headed for Camp Pendleton. We arrived late at night, and we expected the worse. We were waiting for the immortal words, "You have ten seconds to un-ass my marine corps bus!"

Much to our surprise, when we arrived, there were no yellow foot prints, no drill instructor yelling and screaming, just the corporal telling us to go into the barracks, stow our gear, get some sleep, and the first formation will be at 1300 hours the next day. What? We could sleep in, walk to chow for breakfast, take our time eating, go back to the barracks, take a nap, get up, walk to lunch, then form up for training at 1300. Wow, we were all excited. Of course, none of us could sleep in. We got up, cleaned the barracks, got our uniforms together, and waited for something unexpected to happen. It didn't.

At 1300 hours, we formed up. Since I had a stripe, I was made a squad leader by the corporal. We then marched to a large warehouse where we were issued our weapon and 782 gear. That's all your field gear. We marched back to the barracks and were told we were released for the day. We would begin training in the morning with an orientation of what to expect in ITR. We were instructed to put our field gear together as prescribed by standard operating procedure (SOP) and for the squad leaders to inspect their squad before releasing them for the rest of the day for on post liberty. Oh my God, I'd died and gone to Marine heaven. Liberty again!

We knew now that we were in the Marine Corps and what it felt like to be a Marine and to be treated as a Marine for real. We were treated like men, and it was up to us to act like it. By the way, most of us were eighteen and nineteen years old. I was eighteen. I got my gear ready, inspected my squad, and helped a few guys, who looked like they had never done this before. I wondered how the hell they made it through basic training. I instructed them not to get drunk and that curfew was 2100 hours and lights out at 2200 hours. I was getting pretty good at this stuff.

All went well the first day and night. My squad was good to go in the morning, but other squads were not and saw the corporal's anger for the first time that morning. He did not dish out mass punishment, however. He focused on the few duds we had and made the corrections that needed to be made. No punches were thrown, just lots of push-ups.

We were about to receive our first orientation. As we sat in the bleachers waiting for the instructor, we were all wondering when we were going to get our first leave. It was already mid-September, so we figured we'd all be home by mid-October. The instructor came out, and began to go through the sequence of events that would take place in the next four weeks. Then he dropped the bomb. He informed us that after ITR, we would split up again, all going on to what was called BITS, which would be another four weeks of training. *God, we'll never make it home.* BITS was specialty training. We were split into groups of 0311 (grunts), weapons specialists, demolitions specialists, 3.5 rocket launcher trainings, etc. Since I already knew I was a 0311, I now knew I would not be home until around Thanksgiving.

For the next four weeks, our training was actually interesting. The instructors were all returning Vietnam veterans and were trying to teach us not to make the same mistakes they had. They were very professional. One instructor only had one arm. He was in transition waiting to be medically discharged and was assigned to us. He told us he had been blown up by a booby trap, and his left arm was so mangled it had to be amputated. He wanted to stay in the Corps, but they would not allow it. He was an excellent instructor, but was eventually gone. We never saw him again.

The four weeks went by really fast. On graduation day, a colonel congratulated us and wished us well in our continued training. As we returned to our barracks, everyone but the 0311s were told to form up to return their 782 gear to the big warehouse. I asked the corporal why we weren't going, and he said we would be staying there in the same barracks to continue BITS. I, along with the other 0311s, was happy about that. We knew we were in our last phase of training.

BITS

BITS consisted of more advanced Infantry training. We learned basic map reading, communications techniques, patrolling techniques, ambushes, immediate action drills, and basic camouflage techniques. It finished with a three day training exercise designed to simulate a Vietnam type scenario. It was all very interesting, and we knew that learning this, along with a lot of luck, would keep us alive in Vietnam. By now, we were all resigned to the fact that we were headed to Vietnam. As training came to an end, we all were in anticipation of going home on leave. It was nearing the third week of November and almost Thanksgiving. I had been gone since July 11, and it was now November 16. I had been a Marine for four months. I was "salty," (a term used for a seasoned Marine) or at least I thought I was.

Graduation day finally came. We were given our orders the night before and our leave forms. I had twenty-one days of leave. I was assigned to some place called "West Pac." In fact, all of us were. None of us had a clue what that meant. We just knew we were to report back to Camp Pendleton in December to a place called "Staging Battalion." Again, no clue. We cornered the corporal our last night there to talk to him about this West Pac place. He informed us it meant Western Pacific, Vietnam. We weren't shocked. We just couldn't figure out why they just didn't say "Vietnam."

Now I had to tell my family and my girlfriend. I decided I would wait until I got home and tell them in person.

Finally, after what seemed like an eternity, we were headed home for our first leave. It was a Tuesday, two days before Thanksgiving. I remember the day because my girlfriend was in school and could not come to the airport to meet me. I think my mom and aunt picked me up. We spent all day making our flight arrangements, packing up all our gear, just like we were taught in basic training, and headed out to Los Angeles International Airport. I immediately saw small changes in the people around the airport. We were dressed in our dress green uniforms, looking good, but nobody seemed to notice or care. There were small groups of protesters and Hari Krishna's around the airport handing out flowers, but they didn't bother us. We just wanted to get home. It had been over four months since I had any semblance of reality, and I welcomed it.

I had a flight change in Chicago and had about a two hour layover. I sat in a chair just watching the people and enjoying the view, when an army military policeman and his partner approached me. I had unbuttoned my greens jacket to get comfortable and I was out of uniform. I didn't realize it was such a big deal, but the Army MP seemed to think it was. He told me to get to my feet, at which time he began to talk to me like I was back in basic training. He was a sergeant, and I was only a private first class—but I was a Marine, so I decided I was not going to take any crap from a doggy (Army guy). I did correct my uniform, but told him he had no right to talk to me the way he was. He then took me by the arm and told me I was coming with him to the military liaison office. I jerked away from him and told him I had a plane to catch. We were face to face, nobody backing down. His partner didn't seem too interested; he was looking at the girls.

About that time, a Marine gunnery sergeant came up to us and asked what the problem was. I started to explain, but the MP interrupted me and told him I was being detained for insubordination. I had no idea what he was talking about. The Marine gunnery sergeant took the MP aside, and they talked for several minutes. The MPs departed and the gunny came back to me. He told me the Army did not like Marines, and that I was to keep my shit wired, head to my departure gate, and if I saw an Army MP coming my way, to go the other way. I thanked the gunny for his help, and he patted me on the back and said the kindest thing I had heard in over four months. He said, and I will never forget, "Semper fi, Marine." He then smiled at me and departed. Welcome home, gunny.

My flight landed in Columbus, Ohio, and all I wanted to do was get home. It had been a hell of a journey, and I wanted my mom and aunt's home cooking and the loving of my girlfriend. We got home and most of my family had gathered. My oldest brother was there with his new wife and baby; my stepfather and some friends had gathered. I changed my clothes, stored my gear, and waited for all the family to depart before calling my girlfriend to make arrangements to meet. As luck would have it, her dad wanted to see me in uniform, so I had to go back upstairs, find a clean dress shirt, and get back in uniform. A small price to pay to be one of the world's finest. Seeing my girlfriend again was quite an experience. We hugged and kissed right in front of her parents. I was changed, and she and her family noticed immediately. I had matured. I stood up straight, was polite, more so than ever before, and was just plain proud, and they seemed proud of me.

My leave time flew by. I had Thanksgiving at my house and my girlfriend's house. I had to go to my uncle's house, who was a highly decorated medic during the Korean War. I visited my high school and most of my teachers to show them that I had actually done something with myself. I remember my band teacher, Mr. Newman, being extremely proud of me. I stood in front of the band in uniform as he introduced me to the band members I did not know. He asked me what my first assignment would be, and I told him I was headed to Vietnam. I had not told my girlfriend yet, or my family, so she heard it the first time in the band room in front of the entire band. She ran out in tears. I felt terrible that I hadn't told her before then. I guess I assumed they knew. My fault. Another lesson learned—never assume anything.

A few days before my leave was finished, I went to my girlfriend's house to get her for a date. When I got there, she wasn't home. She had gone shopping with a friend of hers to buy me a going away present, but should be home soon. I sat in the kitchen with her mother and had the strangest conversation I had ever had with her. She asked me what my plans were. I didn't understand her question. She then said that my girl would be starting college soon and that things would never be the same between us. I must have had a look of terror on my face because she then grabbed my hand and said, "Nothing is forever." About that time my girl came in the door. She must have seen the look on my face, and immediately asked her mom what she had said to me. Her mother said we were just having a conversation about life. She asked me that night what we were talking about, but I let on that it was just small talk and that her mother was worried about me. I never told her the extent of our conversation.

A conversation came up that night at dinner that I had dreaded since I had come home. I told my family I was headed for Vietnam. My family said they knew; my girlfriend had called and told them. I asked my mom if she had a clue, and she said she figured as much, remembering the conversation with my recruiter.

The day came when I had to leave to go back to Camp Pendleton, California. I had to fly back through Chicago so I decided, in order to avoid any incidents in the airport, I would dress in civilian clothes until I got to California; then I would change into my military uniform before getting a ride to Camp Pendleton. I had a lay-over in Chicago, and didn't want to take a chance on running into the Army MP again. My aunt and my girlfriend took me to the airport. My mom just couldn't stand to see me go. My girlfriend skipped school that day. This seemed like déjà vu. Nearly five months before, my aunt and girlfriend took me to the airport for basic training. This time I would not be home for more than a year, and things would change drastically. Again, kisses were stolen, and I would cop a feel now and again, not thinking my aunt was watching. We got to the airport, and I didn't want them to come in, but they did. I checked in, went to the gate, and waited. My flight was called. I hugged my aunt, kissed my girl, and left. Little did I know, that would be the last time I would ever kiss her.

STAGING BATTALION

Back in the Corps again. After arriving at LAX and changing into my uniform, I went to the military liaison station to catch my ride. There were about twenty other Marines of all ranks waiting. Many were NCO's and Officers returning to Vietnam for a second or third tour. You could tell by the awards and decorations they were wearing. I only had one stripe and one ribbon. Boy, did I feel out of place. About that time, I heard my name being called from across the room. It was one of my friends from basic. We talked the entire way to Camp Pendleton about what we did on leave and worried about what was to become of us next. We arrived with little fanfare and were told to report to a barracks building and stow our gear. They were waiting for another fifty or so Marines to show up to start our processing the next day.

I figured we would have to go through the routine of going to the big warehouse and get field gear, a weapon, and start training again. That was not the case. Staging Battalion was nothing but a clearing station. We processed our files, got our finances straight, and to my surprise, made out a will. Hell, I didn't have anything to leave to anybody, but did what I was told. My life insurance would go to my mother, and all belongings to go to whoever she wanted to give them to. After a couple of days of all of that, we had medical clearances to do. We spent all day taking physicals again, getting our teeth and eyes checked, and yes, getting more shots. Just like in basic training, we were lined up and went through the gauntlet of navy corpsmen, who seemed to enjoy giving us the shots then as much as they did in basic training.

The last day was unit assignments and flight information. Remember in the beginning of the book when I told you there were only two times in my Marine Corps career I got a choice? This was the second and last. We were in formation, about a hundred of us, in front of two buildings. One building had a sign that read, "First Marine Division," and the other had a sign that read, "Third Marine Division." The NCO in charge of our formation told all the officers and other NCO's to fall out; they would be given their assignments individually. All the rest of us were told we had a choice. We were to line up behind one of the signs, first or third. I didn't know anything about either one, neither did my buddy. We kind of stood back watching what everyone was doing. Some made a bee line straight for the division of their choice. I guess they were trying to get back into their old unit, or so I was told. We took a leap of faith and went to the building that said "First Marine Division." This, I would find out later, would be a lifesaving decision. The next day, we packed up all our stuff and went to El Toro Air Force Base, where we were headed to Vietnam. We were told we would land in Okinawa first, then continue on to Vietnam.

While in Staging Battalion, I ran into several guys I had gone to basic training with. There was on guy I'll call PVT Beal. Beal wasn't a very good recruit during basic, and thank God was not in my squad. He only did enough to get by. I remember talking with Beal before we flew out, and he told me he was not going to go to Vietnam. I told him he didn't have a choice. He started acting crazy, but the sergeant in charge kept an eye on him, and he made our plane. While in flight, we were told we would land in Honolulu for a short refuel stop. We were allowed to get off the plane but were told to stay close to our gate because we would only be on the ground for an hour. When we reloaded the plane, the sergeant in charge started checking to make sure everyone was on the plane. Beal was seated about three rows in front of me. His seat was empty. He had gone absent without leave (AWOL). The sergeant asked if any of us had seen him. I kept my mouth shut. I never saw or heard about Beal again. Deserting during time of war is punishable by death. I hope Beal was satisfied with his decision. I looked at it this way: I would not have wanted to be with him in Vietnam. He, more than likely, would have gotten himself or someone else killed. Better he leave now.

OKINAWA

We landed in Okinawa after a flight that seemed like it took forever. We got off the plane, gathered our gear, and were bused to an area called Camp Hansen. Our processing started immediately. No rest. We were given our follow-on flight information and sent to a barracks to get some sleep. My friend and I were on the same plane again going on to Vietnam. We had about a twenty-four hour delay before flying and decided to check out the local Enlisted Man's Club. The beer there was a nickel a cup. I was eighteen and allowed to drink legally. For one dollar, I experienced my first real drunk episode, with accompanying hangover the following morning. I also had to get back on an airplane for the final flight to Vietnam. We must have left the club sometime around midnight. I don't remember. I just know we made it back to the barracks and went to bed. I was on the top bunk and had no idea how I got there. I woke up the next morning with my buddy beating on me. I, at some time during the night, got sick, leaned over the bed and puked right into his boots. I felt really bad. Hangover and all, I had to clean his boots the best I could. We had a flight to catch in a few hours and still had to get cleaned up, get some breakfast, and get to the bus. I couldn't clean his boots well enough, so he made me give him my spare pair of boots, and I had to take his pukey boots. Thank goodness our feet were the same size. I packed the pukey boots in my sea bag. My sea bag smelled like puke for the next year.

We went to breakfast. I almost threw up again looking at the scrambled eggs and greasy bacon. I think I managed to get some toast and juice down, and started to feel better. My next mission, find some aspirin. I found a navy corpsman that was on our flight in the barracks. He was packing his aid bag and it looked like he had some medical supplies with him. I asked (more like begged) for him to give me something.

He said, "You guys will never learn," and proceeded to give me two little blue pills.

I had no idea what they were and didn't care. I took them and left. We got on our plane and took off, none the worse for wear. I promptly fell asleep. I woke up an hour or two into the flight, hungry as hell. The flight attendant, called a stewardess back then, was handing out meals. I ate mine and tried to take my buddy's, but he wouldn't let me.

The plane got quiet again and I fell back asleep. I woke up to the pilot coming on the intercom announcing that if we looked out the left side of the cabin we could see the coast of Vietnam. We would be landing shortly.

Then he said, "Welcome to Vietnam!"

CHAPTER 5

KILO COMPANY

THIRD BATTALION, SEVENTH MARINES

396 DAYS AND A WAKE UP

Staging Battalion
December 1967

You'll never get a Purple Heart hiding in a foxhole! Follow me!

— Captain Henry P Crowe, USMC

As the plane started its descent into Vietnam, we noticed the plane didn't seem to slow down much. All of a sudden, the plane went into a steep angle of descent, giving us the feeling the plane was about to crash. Then, the pilot leveled off and the wheels touched the ground. He applied heavy brakes and we all lurched forward. We couldn't figure out what was happening, then an officer next to us told us the Viet Cong would sometimes shoot at the planes, and mortar the runway when planes would arrive, so the pilot wasn't taking any chances. We were glad the pilot had done this before. We taxied over to a hanger and waited. A few minutes went by and the door opened. I was about half way back in the plane and couldn't really tell what was going on. An Air Force sergeant entered the plane and got on the intercom. He told the officers and senior NCO's to go to the hanger on the right and for everyone else to go to the hanger on the left.

As people started to shuffle off the plane, we didn't know what to expect. When we finally started moving, our sense of anticipation grew. When I got to the door, all I can remember was the heat and the smell. I had never experienced such heat and foul smell in my entire life. The smell was a combination of jet fuel and sewer, all mixed together. It was one huge, hot, steamy, smelly sewer. How in the hell was I going to get used to this? By the time we got to the hanger, we were all sweating bullets. Our utility uniforms were soaked with sweat. I couldn't believe how hot it was, and it was December. The exact date was 16 December 1967. I was eighteen years old, in a foreign country, about to begin the journey and the fight of my life.

We were all looking for some water to drink. An NCO pointed out a large green bag hanging from a large tri-pod. He said water was in it. It was called a Lister bag. There were no cups, so we would have to use the buddy system to get the water out. One person would press down on the drain, while the other cupped his hands and drank the water. We stood in line and finally got up to drink. The water was so warm you could take a bath in it and didn't taste much better. It was filling though, and at that point, beggars' couldn't be choosers. Finally, the Air Force NCO came in with a bull horn so everyone could hear him. He sent all the Marines to a barracks in one direction, and all other services in another direction. We were assigned to what amounted to a tent with wooden sides on it with cots inside. We were told to wait there for further instructions. We were trying to find the tent with the air conditioner, but it was not to be. The ones with the air conditioners belonged to the officers and senior NCO's. We had to gut it out. That's why they call us grunts I guess. We made ourselves as comfortable as possible and waited.

When we got off the plane, we had handed the Air Force guy one copy of our orders. About an hour went by, when a Marine corporal came into our tent with those orders in his hand. He was dressed in starched jungle fatigues and a cover. He was tanned and looked like he had just stepped out of a movie poster. He stated that each day at noon, he would post assignments for everyone. There were a couple of days delay because so many Marines were arriving now; that's why we were in tents, not barracks. He said to check the board every day at noon to see what units we would go to. Once that was done, we would find the perspective clerk for that unit, and he would arrange transportation. He said we would probably be there for three or four days. After he was done, I asked him where we would draw our field equipment, weapons, and jungle fatigues. I was shocked when he told me we would get all of that when we arrived at our new unit. What? We're in a combat zone, and no weapon? He said it was pretty secure there and not to worry. That night it felt like I was sleeping in a steam bath. It was hot, muggy, smelly, no breeze at all. Most guys had stripped down to their skivvies by now, so I did the same. Sleep was restless that night, but I did manage to fall off several times, only to be awakened by the sound of F-4 phantom jets taking off down the runway during the night on the way to bail out some grunt company in contact with the enemy.

I woke up the next morning lying in my own sweat. What a miserable night. The same corporal came in and told us we would be moving into the barracks after evening chow. It would be air conditioned and a lot more comfortable. He also needed a detail of five Marines. Even though I was always told not to volunteer for anything, I did. I was bored and needed something to do. I couldn't believe it when he gave me and the other four suckers brushes and a five gallon bucket of white paint and told us to paint every rock in camp white. For some reason, they had this obsession with painting rocks around there. I made a mental note to myself, *Don't volunteer for anything again!* My orders were not posted that day, so I waited for the word to move to the new barracks. Finally, around 1900 hours, we were told to move. We found our barracks okay, but found the air conditioner to be just two big fans, one on each side of the room. All they did was blow hot air. *Well, better than nothing, I guess.*

The next day, the friend that I had been with all this time got his orders. He was going to Fifth Marines. The same unit our corporal at ITR had come from. We were sorry he couldn't remember the corporal's name so my friend could ask anybody there if they knew him. I never saw my friend again. I am sorry to say, I don't remember his name either.

That's sad if you think about it. I remember my SDI and ADI's names, and also all the guys who did bad things, but not the friend I flew over there with. I don't know if he made it back or not. Welcome home, my friend.

The next day, I got my assignment. I was going to Third Battalion, Seventh Marines. Nobody there knew much about the unit other than it was about twenty-five miles from Da Nang. I gathered with a bunch of other Marines and found another guy I had gone to basic training with. Sam was in the same series as I was, but not in platoon 3028. I just remembered seeing him. We started talking; he had just flown in the day before. He laughed at me when he asked what I had been doing since I got there and told him I had been painting rocks. We went to the briefing tent to get our records looked at and to make final transportation arrange- ments when we got the next big surprise. During the briefing by the personnel people, they informed us the Marines did not serve a twelve month tour like everyone else, we served a thirteen month tour. Good God, thirty extra days. They never did explain why the Marines did a thirteen month tour, but my lot was not to question why. Everyone counted the days until their return home. I had been in Vietnam for two days, only 394 days to go.

Transportation to our unit would be there the next morning. They said we should pack our gear the night before, go to breakfast, then come to the briefing tent and wait. We asked about going out into town that night. We had been told to go to this place called "Dog Patch." This was where the bars and steam baths were. We couldn't figure out why anyone would want to go to a steam bath. It was 110 degrees in the shade with 100 percent freaking humidity. Hell we lived in a steam bath. The clerk in the tent advised us not to go into Dog Patch. He said we were new and the crooks down there would know we were new and steal our money. As far as the steam bath goes, it was a front for a whore house. He said if we went, to use rubbers because they had all kind of bad diseases down there.

There was one story they told us about the diseases I will never forget. One was called the "black syphilis." They said if you get it, it cannot be cured and you are sent off to an island somewhere to live the rest of your life. It was said to be worse than leprosy. I knew it was a myth, but I didn't take any chances. Bill and I went to the make-shift enlisted man's club, drank a couple of beers and went back to the barracks for the night. We decided going into Dog Patch just wasn't worth the risk.

Again, the night was spent in restless sleep. We would hear the occasional F-4 phantom jet take off and wonder if, in the near future, one would be taking off to come to protect or save us. That would be true on more than one occasion in the next thirteen months. We woke the next morning, took a quick shower, dressed, and went to breakfast. The breakfast there wasn't that terrible. I remember having eggs to order, crisp bacon, even a waffle. I didn't drink coffee then, but I had cold water with ice in it—the last I would have in a very long time. Sam and I returned to the barracks to pack our bags and get ready for the trip to our new unit. We were both excited to get going. Excitement fueled by fear was the order of the day.

At about 1000 hours, a big truck came rumbling up to the staging area where everyone waited for transportation. It had a driver in it and on top was a .50 caliber machine gun mounted on a ring mount that could shoot in a 360 degree direction. Both Marines were covered in dust and wore bandanas over their mouths and noses. They looked like something out of a movie. The driver yelled out for anyone going to third of the seventh to load up; they would be leaving as soon as the two of them got a cold soda and went to the head. There were six of us going to third of the seventh: one very young looking lieutenant, three Sergeants, and Sam and me. The sergeants were returning from rest and relaxation (R&R) and the lieutenant was new like us. While we waited for the driver to come back, we asked the sergeants what it was like. Two of them didn't pay any attention to us, the other just said for us to watch the guys who had been in country for a while and to not do anything stupid.

He said, "Just keep your shit wired and you'll be okay."

That was the second time in my short Marine Corps career that someone had told me to keep my shit wired. The driver and gunner came back and told us we were about to leave. It would be about an hour drive to Hill 37, where the battalion was stationed. They also said that if the shit hit the fan to get down in the bed of the truck and not look up. We noticed that there were filled sand bags in the bed of the truck. They would protect anyone in the back of the truck in case we hit a land mine on the road. This was getting scarier by the minute.

The trip to Hill 37 went off without incident. We traveled down a dirt road filled with civilians along the way. The truck driver was driving so fast it was a wonder he didn't hit anybody. He had driven the route so many times, I guess he was used to it. The final leg of the trip took us across a river. The bridge was guarded at both ends by Marines. In the next year, I would spend many days and nights guarding that bridge. We could see Hill 37 now, and it looked like something out of years past. We could see tents lined up and a huge old French bunker with lots of antennas on top of it.

The hill seemed very large. We would later find out that our Infantry battalion, a tank company, and an artillery detachment were on the hill. We pulled up to a tent with a red sign with yellow letters on it that read, "S-1. Welcome to 3/7."

The driver got out, lowered the tail gate of the truck, and told us to get out there. We got out, and he just drove off leaving Sam and me and the young lieutenant just standing there. The three Sergeants walked off in different directions. The lieutenant introduced himself as Second Lieutenant Mayo. He obviously was new to the battalion, too. We stood there a few minutes when a lance corporal came out of the tent. He told the 2LT to report inside to the adjutant and for us to stand by. He returned inside, and we took a seat on our sea bags and waited. He returned a few minutes later and took our files. He told me that I was assigned to Kilo Company, and Sam was assigned to Mike Company. He told us to report to the respective company tents and showed us where to go. Then he asked if either of us knew how to type. I had taken typing in school but didn't know if that mattered, so I kept my mouth shut. I guess it was the whole thing about not volunteering. Sam said he could type, so the clerk told me to move out to Kilo Company and told Sam to come into the S-1 tent. I found out later that Sam was assigned to S-1 as a clerk/typist. He would not have to go to Mike Company after all. Sometimes it pays to volunteer, I guess.

I went to a tent that had a sign similar to the one outside the S-1 that read, "Kilo 3/7." I assumed I was in the right place. I knocked loudly on the screen door, as I was taught in basic training to do, and waited.

A voice from inside yelled, "You don't have to knock. Come on in!"

I went in and it was stifling hot in there. A fan was going, but only managed to push the hot air around. There were two clerks at small green desks typing away at something. One of the clerks stood up and introduced himself as PFC Bock. Bock told me the other guy's name, but he didn't bother to look up or say anything. Bock would become one of my very good friends. Bock told me he was expecting me and to have a seat. It was lunch time by then and he said he was just about to go to the chow hall for lunch and asked if I wanted to come with him. He said we would finish up my paperwork after lunch. I figured it would be a good time to ask some questions and get any information I could about the company.

We went to the chow hall (another tent) and I was very surprised at how different the food was. It was horrible. All they had to drink was green Kool-Aid and warm water. I, to this day, cannot drink green Kool-Aid. We sat and made small talk, and he asked me where I was from in "the world." I told him Zanesville, Ohio. He'd never heard of it. He was from somewhere in Florida, I think. He said Kilo Company was presently on Hill 55, Seventh Marine Regimental Headquarters hill. It was Kilo Company's turn for the security detail on that hill. They would pull hole watch (guard duty) at night, run some night ambushes (small unit patrols during the day to the village below the hill), but no extended operations. He said it was pretty cushy duty for the grunts and a chance to get their shit re-wired. *There's that saying again. I guess everyone over here says that. Note to self: keep your shit wired.*

We continued the small talk and I asked him if Kilo was a good company. He said he thought it had some of the best officers and NCO's in the battalion. He said I should be glad I wasn't assigned to India Company; they seemed to always get their asses kicked every time they left the wire. Kilo had sustained casualties, however. Just a week prior, they had three Marines killed in action. I would probably be replacing one of those Marines. That was unsettling to say the least. I was going to a squad who had lost a fellow Marine. Would they accept me? Could I meet the expectations of their fallen comrade? My questions would soon be answered.

After lunch we returned to the orderly room.

Bock said I would be going to third platoon, where the platoon sergeant would assign me to a squad. I would stay on Hill 37 for a couple of days to get acclimated to the heat, draw my weapon, uniforms, and equipment, and to pull hole watch at night.

I was anxious to get to the company, but he told me not to worry, "You'll get your chance."

I grabbed my gear and followed him up the hill to our company tents. There would be a couple of Marines there from the company. Two were waiting to go home, and two or three had gotten there a day or two prior and were waiting to meet up with the company. Others were there recuperating from wounds and waiting to go back to the company, also. He told me to grab a bunk, stow my gear and return in about an hour to the orderly room, and he would take me to supply to draw my gear.

I entered the tent. The sides of the tent were rolled up to allow air to move around and it was dirty, dusty, and hot. I thought, *This is going to be a long thirteen months.* The two Marines headed home were taking naps. They looked older than they actually were, tanned, worn out, and scruffy looking.

They looked like they had been through hell, and in fact, they had. Four of the guys were playing cards. One of the wounded guys was also taking a nap. He had a bandage on his upper arm and another on his chest. I found out later he had been hit with shrapnel from the same booby trap that killed some other Marines the week prior. He told me later that he only had about a month to go and hoped he wouldn't have to go back to the field. I totally understood. He would return to first platoon, but they kept him in the platoon area. He didn't have to go back out to the bush.

I was learning more and more about Kilo Company as the day went on. I found out they were salty Marines, not afraid to take the fight to the enemy. The company clerk told me my platoon leader's name. Bock told me he was the best in the company and well-liked by the platoon. I was excited to meet him. The platoon sergeant was a staff sergeant. I would learn later not to piss him off, but I would get in trouble first and feel his wrath.

Bock took me to supply where I met the supply sergeant. He issued me an M14, which was cool because it had a bi-pod and an automatic selector on it, meaning I could fire it on full automatic. Awesome firepower. The only problem was that he had no ammo pouches for the magazines. He gave me an ammo can with about ten M14 magazines with it. Also, the flack vest he gave me had dried blood on it. He told me I should wash it off because it would draw bugs. Good God, everything drew bugs around there. The only good things issued were brand new jungle fatigues, two brand new pairs of jungle boots, and a new booney hat. He also gave me four new pairs of socks and four brand new olive green t-shirts. I asked if I was going to get new skivvies, too.

He said "No, you won't need them; nobody wears skivvies over here."

I was confused. He said I would learn why later, but I should take the skivvies I had and make cleaning rags for my weapon out of them. I had about an hour before chow when I got back to the tent.

The two guys going home were up now and seemed very interested in the new guys. I had not been introduced to anyone yet, so it was time to meet my fellow Kilo Marines. One of the guys going home came over to me and told me he would help me get my shit together. He had been told I was going to third platoon. He told me he had just left "Third Herd" and he didn't want me showing up there looking like "Joe shit the rag man." That was the first time I had heard the platoon referred to as Third Herd, and I didn't know who Joe shit the rag man was, so I asked him. He laughed and told me it was just something his drill instructor had called him during basic training. I told him I wasn't called anything that nice in basic. We had a good laugh out of it. I asked him why nobody wore skivvies. He told me when we wore skivvies; the heat and sweat would cause a terrible rash, and getting rid of the skivvies would keep us from getting the rash. Good enough for me. I didn't wear skivvies again for the next twenty-five years.

We went to chow and he filled me in on the rest of the platoon. He told me Third Squad was under investigation for the rape and murder of a young Vietnamese girl from one of the villages outside of Hill 55. The squad had been on an ambush the same night she came up missing. A day later, her body was found in a well. Third squad was the only squad in that area, so they were being investigated. He told me it probably wasn't them. The Viet Cong would come into the villages at night and commit unspeakable crimes in the villages and that was probably what had happened. He told me that all the new guys were looked upon very suspiciously. There had been information passed to the company that Criminal Investigation Division (CID) agents had been planted in the squads acting like new guys to gain information about black market activities, drugs, murders, rapes of civilians, and other illegal activities. He told me not to be surprised if everyone treated me poorly for a little while until they got to know me.

I told him, "Look, I'm barely eighteen years old, never shaved in my life before basic training, and didn't even know what a CID agent was!"

He told me it didn't matter what I looked like, everyone was suspicious of FNG's, especially since an investigation was on-going. When I ask what an FNG was, I learned it was: Fucking New Guy.

That night I was assigned hole watch duty with another new Marine. We were both on edge; it was our first duty as combat Marines. Early in the evening a lieutenant came by our hole and told us we were on 100 percent alert and that no one was allowed to sleep. Like we could anyway. He said that an attack on our position was imminent, and to be on the lookout. He told us not to fire on anything, but to use the field telephone in the bunker and call for him or the sergeant of the guard and they would come and check it out. Holly crap, I was scared out of my mind. My first night on watch, and we're about to be attacked. Both of us stayed awake all night long. When it got dark, you couldn't see your hand in front of your face. Every noise sounded like an entire regiment of Viet

Cong coming at you. Of course, we didn't know what that sounded like anyway, but we imagined.

Sometime around midnight, the artillery detachment started firing. It scared the holly be-jesus out of us. Nobody had hollered "fire in the hole" like we were taught in basic training to warn us something was about to happen. I think I soiled myself, but I'm not sure. This went on for about five minutes. About that time, the sergeant of the guard showed up. He hollered at us to let us know he was coming into the bunker and not to shoot him. He knew we were newbies and didn't want to get killed by one of us. He told us the artillery was firing in support of a mission going on in the Arizona territory—an area I would soon become very familiar with.

The Arizona territory was a very bad place. It was a Viet Cong and a North Vietnamese strong hold. He also said one of us could go to sleep while the other stayed awake for the rest of the night. Are you kidding me? Neither one of us could sleep now. During the night, the artillery continued to fire missions into the Arizona. Every now and then, the mortars would fire illumination rounds into the air and light up the night. We would watch very closely in our area of responsibility. Every time an illumination round would go off, we thought we saw movement. We kept the officer in charge and the NCO that night on their toes. We must have called them five times that night. They weren't mad, but each time we called, one of them had to come to the hole and check it out. Of course, we didn't see anything; it was only our imagination that we were being attacked by the entire North Vietnamese army (NVA).

The night ended uneventfully, and we were relieved in the morning. We were told to go to chow and then report to the orderly room for details. I thought to myself, *Wait, we've been up all night. Don't we get to rest?* No. After chow we reported to Bock in the orderly room and met our company commander. I don't remember his name, but he had just flown in from Hill 55 for a meeting with the battalion commander. He welcomed us to Kilo Company and told us if we needed anything to let him know. He was a personable enough guy, and we thought we were lucky to be in Kilo. Bock told us we would be going to Hill 55 in the morning. The supply sergeant had a detail for us that would last until lunch and then we would be released for the rest of the day to get our shit together for the ride to Hill 55 the next day. We went to the supply room to find the supply sergeant with a can of paint and two paint brushes. Yes, we were going to paint rocks again. *Why the hell is the Marine Corps obsession with painting rocks?*

About that time, the company commander came running into the supply tent and told him to forget about area beautification for the time being. A bunch of helicopters were about to arrive with dead and wounded Marines from the action the night before and every available Marine was to report to the LZ (landing zone). We dropped the paint brushes and all of us, along with the company commander and supply sergeant, ran to the LZ. A few minutes later, we heard helicopters coming.

There seemed to be a bunch of them, but there were only three. The first two were full of wounded Marines. We ran aboard and grabbed the end of a litter and took them to the waiting vehicles. I couldn't look down at their faces. I was too scared of what I might see. The last one came in with the dead Marines and the equipment picked up on the battlefield.

They also had a wounded Viet Cong (VC) on the helicopter. We unloaded the body bags. Thank God they were in body bags—that way I didn't have to look. That might sound like a cold statement, but I don't think I was ready to see my first dead Marine yet.

We then unloaded what seemed like a lot of equipment. All of the equipment was bloody and a mess. They took the wounded VC off on a litter and laid him beside the LZ. No effort was made to take him to the aid station. My company commander told me and the other Marine to stay with him; someone from headquarters would be down shortly to get him. He was horribly wounded, but still alive. I don't know how, but he was. We stood there looking at him as his breath became more and more shallow. A few minutes later, about four Marines and one Vietnamese came to the LZ. The Vietnamese soldier bent down and began talking to him. I had no idea what he was saying, but I figured he was trying to interrogate him. A few minutes later, the VC prisoner died. It was the first time I had ever seen someone die, but not the last. I didn't feel bad. He was the enemy. We were told to take him on the litter to a waiting jeep, then report back to our company area. We didn't really notice until we got back to the company area, but we had dried blood all over us. The supply sergeant told us we were a mess and to go to the latrine and get cleaned up. Oh my God, 390 days and a wake up.

We cleaned ourselves up and were told we would not have to do anything else the rest of the day, and to secure and go get our shit together for our ride tomorrow. We didn't realize it, but we were beat. When we got back to the hootch (tent), we both laid down on our racks and passed out. We were awakened by the Marine who was about to go home. He said we slept right through lunch. It was dinner time now, and he suggested we get up and go to chow. We thanked him and got up.

We walked to chow with him, and he told us he was leaving in the morning for "the world." He said he couldn't wait to get back to the land of the big PX. We wished we were him. He told us he had been in country for eighteen months. He extended his tour so he could be discharged as soon as he got home and wouldn't have to spend any more time in the Marine Corps than he had to. I couldn't believe it. He had been in Vietnam since June 1966. I was still in high school in 1966. He seemed years older than us, but in reality, he was only twenty years old. He was a really nice guy and tried to help us the best he could. He told us he had been wounded twice. Who else to listen to than someone who had been in country for the last eighteen months and wounded twice? I don't remember his name, but he probably goes to our reunions. Welcome home, Marine.

That evening we packed our bags up again. We would turn in our sea bags with all of the gear we were issued in basic training to supply the next morning. We would not need it for thirteen months. All we owned was what we carried. Our rucksacks were packed full. We were issued a foot locker to keep our personal gear in like pictures, letters and other stuff we didn't want to take to the bush. That night, the Marine who was leaving gave us one last word of advice. He told us to gather up as many canteens we could get our hands on. He said he always carried four. We were only issued two. He said we could never drink enough water.

That night, we didn't draw hole watch duty. We had the night off. Somewhere around midnight, I was awakened to a deafening sound of explosions on the hill. This was a new sound to me, and it didn't sound like the outgoing artillery fire like the night before. The Marine that was going home the next day started yelling, "Incoming!" He told us to grab our shit and get in the bunker outside the tent. I hadn't really paid attention, but there was a small bunker outside each tent. They were designed to jump into at the first sound of incoming, then move to the perimeter. As we dove into the bunker, we seemed to run over more people doing the same thing. People cussed and yelled. Finally, the home bound Marine yelled for me and the other newbie to follow him.

Explosions were still going off, but on another side of the hill. He knew that and told us to run to the perimeter with him. We ran in the dark; the only light was the light from the explosions. My right foot hit a hole and I tumbled and fell out of control. I got up and continued to run. I got to the perimeter bunker and the sergeant asked me if I was hit. I told him I didn't know, but my right ankle was killing me. He took out his handy Zippo lighter (a very important piece of equipment that I found out everyone needed, even if we didn't smoke) to see if I was wounded. I had sprained my ankle really bad. I could feel it swelling in my boot. He told me not to remove my boot because if I did, I would never get it back on. I was scared.

The explosions seemed to stop as fast as they started. He said we had been rocketed. I found out the enemy had sent 122 mm rockets onto our hill, a common occurrence. The 122 mm rocket was very lethal. Finally, we secured and returned to our hootch. The Marine said he couldn't believe he was going to be killed his last night on Hill 37 after spending eighteen months in the Nam and being wounded twice. He told me to go to the battalion aid station to have my ankle checked out.

I limped to the battalion aid station, and there was flurry of activity around it. Some Marines had been wounded, and they were caring for them. I felt bad; I only had a sprained ankle and returned to my hootch. He asked what I was doing back, and I told him. He said to make sure I had it checked out in the morning before we moved to Hill 55. I did not take my boot off that night.

The next morning, I woke to my ankle killing me. I got up and limped to the aid station. I was the first one up. At the aid station, the corpsman took off my boot to look at my ankle. It started swelling before my very eyes. It hurt like hell. He had the battalion surgeon come over and look at it. He said it didn't look broken and told the corpsman to wrap it and put me on three days bed rest. I was not happy. I was supposed to go to Hill 55 that morning. How was it going to look to my new platoon with me lying in my rack for three days while they were in the bush? I felt really bad. I put my boot back on, limped to the chow, and saw the other newbie. Asking how I was, I told him my situation.

He told me, if it were him, he would go on to Hill 55. I asked where the Marine that was going home was and learned he had flown out on the first helicopter that morning to Da Nang, headed home. I felt bad. I hoped all the Marines I would soon meet would be like him. I wanted to thank him for all he had done for us in the last two days. I limped back to our hootch thinking about my predicament. I hadn't told the company clerk what had happened yet, and decided to play macho Marine and go on to Hill 55 with the rest of the guys going that morning. I tied my boot up as tight as I could get it, grabbed my gear and hobbled down to the orderly room to catch our ride. I was in pain the entire way.

Six Marines were waiting for the truck to Hill 55. Bock came up to us, wished us luck, and said he would see us soon. He also asked why I was limping. I told him it was no big deal. He said he knew what had happened, the departing Marine told him that morning before he caught his ride to Da Nang. He had told Bock to watch out for me, that I was hurting. Bock said if I wanted to stay behind, I could. I told him no thanks, I wanted to go. Bock then said, "Semper Fi," and we loaded up and departed for Hill 55.

Pvt. Donald G. Tackett
Home on leave
November 1967

CHAPTER 6

CHRISTMAS, 1967

Ho Ho, BOOM!

Come on you sons of bitches, do you want to live forever!

— Gunnery Sergeant Dan Daley, USMC

Belleau Woods, 1918

As I begin to write this chapter, it is Christmas 2011. Forty-four years earlier, I spent my first Christmas ever away from home. It was 25 December 1967. I'd never been away from home for Christmas, or any other holiday for that matter. I don't really remember Christmas day. By then, all the days were running together—and I had only been in Vietnam a little more than a week. I do remember spending Christmas Eve on hole watch. I was envisioning another mortar or rocket attack that night and remembered I would much rather be in this bunker than in a tent. Rockets and mortars were lethal weapons used by our enemy to disrupt our night and quite frankly, to scare the hell out of us. Guess what? It worked.

I also must say from this point on in the book, I am not just relying on my memory of events that took place, but on the memories of others in Kilo Third of the Seventh who have added their versions of certain events. I will be the first to admit my memory isn't what it used to be, so to depict these events as accurately as possible, I have asked other Marines from Kilo to assist. I have talked to many members of Kilo who attend our reunions, and they have gladly given their input. Many wish to remain anonymous, and I will respect their wishes. I have also changed the names of many Marines in the book to avoid undue embarrassment or ridicule. These events are portrayed as accurately as I can possibly get them, and if I have, by mistake, misrepresented any event in the rest of the book, then I am truly sorry.

Our trip to Hill 55 would take us down what was called Liberty Road. It was called that because after the road dog-legged left it continued to Hill 55. If we went straight we ended up at Liberty Bridge which crossed the river that led into the Arizona Territory. It was the only bridge that crossed the river to the only road that led to An Hoa, another Marine outpost. I would spend a lot of time on Liberty Bridge, and that would be where my life and the lives of many others would change forever. The big truck showed up, it seemed to be the same truck that picked us up in Da Nang earlier. They all looked the same, though. It had the ring mounted .50 caliber machine gun on it with a driver and a gunner, both with the same bandanas over their faces. I needed one of those bandanas.

The driver briefed us that the road was not secure. Trucks and convoys had been ambushed, and the road was sometimes mined. He would haul ass as fast as the truck would take us. We had been issued ammo and were told to lock and load once we left the perimeter gate onto the road. We were also placed in the bed of the truck facing out to protect and to be able to shoot if needed. I was placed sitting on the bed of the truck on my rucksack on the rear looking back. We were all nervous; everybody said they hated the trip down Liberty Road. The trip should only take about thirty minutes, but that was enough time for bad things to happen. Most of the time, it would happen at the dog-leg because the truck had to slow down to make the turn.

As we left the safety of Hill 37, I remember looking back thinking that I kind of liked it there and couldn't wait for the company to get back. We all were given the command to lock and load and we were off. As the truck picked up speed, I looked out to the sides of the road and saw lush vegetation. The jungle had been cleared back about fifty feet it seemed on both sides. Later on in my tour, we would see planes passing low over the jungle applying a defoliate that was called Agent Orange. Agent Orange killed all the vegetation it came into contact with and got rid of hiding places the enemy could use to ambush us.

We were about twenty minutes into the trip when the gunner announced we were coming up to the dog-leg in the road and to be on the lookout. That definitely would not be a problem. Suddenly, I heard a .50 caliber cut loose. It sounded like a cannon going off. The gunner then yelled, "Ambush right!" meaning we were taking fire from the right side of the road. Everyone on the right side of the vehicle opened up with their weapons. I looked out the back and cut loose on full automatic with my M14 rifle. It was the first time I had ever shot at anyone, but not the last. Before I realized it, I was out of ammo. I grabbed my metal ammo box with my other magazines in it and struggled to get the box open. *Note to self: open can before leaving perimeter from now on.* I got it open and changed magazines.

Then the truck hit a big hole in the road, and my helmet went flying out of the back of the truck. The guy to my right saw it and kept trying to shove me down to the bed of the truck. I kept getting back up so I could continue to fire. The truck slowed and made the dog-leg turn. The firing ceased, and we continued on up to Hill 55. I never saw the enemy who was firing at us. Most of the time, we never saw who we were firing at. To enter Hill 55, we had to cross a bridge again. The tower at the bridge had heard the firing and alerted the commander. He had already activated a reaction force to come help out if we needed it. The truck driver did a hell of a job driving through the ambush and acted like it was just another day at the office.

He stopped the truck at our final destination, got out, lowered the tail gate, and asked if we were all okay. Nobody had been hit, but the truck had about ten to twenty bullet holes in it—all near the front of the truck. Had the enemy had better aim, he would have definitely hit one or two of us (if not more) because he did manage to hit the truck. The only damage I sustained was to my ego: I had lost my helmet. I was not only hurting with my ankle injury, but would now have to explain how I lost my helmet. Not a good start with my new platoon sergeant. Only a little over a week in country, and I had already been mortared, rocketed, and shot at. This was about to become interesting. I had reacted properly and did not hide from the shots being fired at us. I guess it all happened so fast, we really didn't have time to think about it—we just reacted as we were trained.

The driver knew my ankle was hurt and helped me off the truck. He asked where my helmet was, and I told him what happened. He said, "Don't worry about it. It happens all the time." I was more worried about what my platoon sergeant was going to say. I was the only one going to third platoon, so he told me where the tent was and we said our good-byes. I hobbled to the tent, which was nearby, dropped my gear outside, and went in. There were two Marines sitting on bunks in the tent. I told them who I was and that I was a new replacement. They said the platoon sergeant and platoon commander would be back soon and most of the squads were out on patrols. They told me to take a seat and wait.

I guess I must have nodded off because I was awakened by someone nudging me, asking who I was. The other two guys had left, and I was alone in the tent. It was my new platoon sergeant. He introduced himself and told me to follow him, so I got up, limping, and followed him to the back of the tent. He asked what was wrong with my leg and I had to explain. Then I had to drop the bomb that I had lost my helmet on the ride in when we were ambushed. He told me it wasn't a problem and to get my soft cover out and wear it. He also told me I was going to be assigned to third squad. He told me about the investigation going on with the squad and the alleged rape and murder the squad was suspected of. The squad had been taken into Da Nang earlier that morning to be questioned by the CID about the incident. He said they would be back the next day. In the meantime, I would report to first squad. He asked if my ankle was okay, and I said it was, even though it hurt like hell.

I went to regimental supply to get a new helmet and then to go to chow. I was surprised he didn't ask any questions about the ambush, but figured it was just old news to him. He had been in country about nine months by now and had seen more than his fair share of ambushes.

I limped to supply and met up with a couple of guys I had been in the truck with. They had also been sent there to get extra equipment. I got a new helmet and asked for more canteens, but he said he didn't have any. The other two guys and I went on to chow. The food was actually pretty good there, but all they had to drink was that damn green Kool-Aid again. I ate and returned to the tent. The platoon sergeant told me where to go, just a few tents away, and wait for first squad to get back from patrol.

I went in the tent and waited. I straightened out my equipment, put my new helmet together, and promptly fell asleep on an empty rack. I don't know how long I was out, but I was awakened by someone kicking the rack telling me I was in his rack. I got up to see the squad I had been temporarily assigned to had just returned. They looked salty. The guy that woke me showed me an empty rack and told me to put my gear there.

He said the squad leader was being debriefed by the platoon commander, but should be back soon. The guy talking to me became one of my good friends. His name was Mike, and he was from Indiana. Another guy came up and introduced himself as David, from Massachusetts. Both were very friendly and told me they would help me get my shit together. I told them I was only with them until third squad got back.

They kind of looked at each other and one of them said, "Well, that could be a long time!"

I was shocked. I didn't know what he meant. He told me the investigation was going to take some time, and if the investigation found they might have done it they would be kept in Da Nang for trial. I didn't know what to say and kept my thoughts to myself.

Dave and Mike were jokesters. I found out quickly they liked to play practical jokes on the new guys, and I wouldn't be exempt. The squad leader, Bill, from New York, finally came back from his briefing. I introduced myself, and he told me not to get comfortable, that I would be going to third squad when they returned from Da Nang. Not new news for me, but I said, "Yes corporal," and just stood there. He started cleaning his weapon and looked up at me as if I knew what I was supposed to do. Of course, I had no idea. He told me to go get my shit together, that we would be on hole watch after evening chow. I did what I was told and hung close to Dave and Mike. The others didn't seem to want to have anything to do with me. We made small talk and they asked about my ankle. I said it was okay, and we went to chow.

Everybody was really nervous about being up on the Regimental Hill. There were a lot of big brass (officers) up there just waiting to find a grunt out of uniform to mess with. I was told to keep my shit together, always have a cover on and my weapon with me at all times. They also had this thing about keeping their boots shined. What? I wasn't quite sure why, but I tried my best. It was difficult, to say the least, because of all the dust when it was dry and all the mud when it was wet.

After chow, it was time for what was called guard mount. It was a procedure that included inspecting our gear and weapons, making sure everyone knew the special orders of the day, and the challenge and password for the night. As we were preparing for guard mount the jokesters, Dave and Mike, told me to go up to the platoon sergeant and ask if we were to take our boot polish up to hole watch with us. Of course it was a joke, but I was a lowly PFC, so I did what I was told. The platoon sergeant was standing with our lieutenant, whom I hadn't met yet, when I approached. He ask what I wanted, so I ask about the boot polish on hole watch. The lieutenant starting cracking up laughing, but the platoon sergeant didn't see the humor. He called me a smart ass and told me when we got off hole watch tomorrow he had a special detail for a smart ass like me.

I hadn't even met the lieutenant yet and was already being yelled at in front of him. Not a good way to start. I went back to guard mount with the entire squad laughing at me. They called me several names like FNG, cherry, and newbie. I knew then, I had been had by the jokesters. I would not let that happen again. I was assigned hole watch with Mike and Dave. We had a good laugh about the joke until the next day when I had to report for my detail.

We had an uneventful night on hole watch. The artillery did fire several fire missions into the Arizona Territory, but that was about it. The next morning we were relieved of our duties and told to go to breakfast, then go get some sleep. The squad leader said we would be going out that night on a squad size ambush. Okay, my first time on patrol, and it's going to be at night. I was scared to death. After chow, my squad leader told me I had to report to the platoon sergeant for detail, no sleep for me. I was expecting it, but was hoping he forgot all about the boot polish incident. Not to be. I banged on the door of his hootch and he told me to enter. He took me and two other newbie's down to an area by the latrines. The latrines were nothing more than outside toilets. They had doors in the back that opened. Under the holes where you did your business were fifty-five gallon drums cut in half. They were filled with a combination of gasoline and diesel fuel. It kept down the smell and the bugs. Every day, someone would have to drag them out of the back of the head, drag them to an open area, add a little more gasoline, and light it. We would then stand over the burning mess with a long stick and stir until all the excrement had turned to ash. We would then fill new drums with the mixture and replace it under the hole. This process continued until all the latrines were finished.

I looked around Hill 55 and there seemed to be fifty or more latrines. I thought to myself: *I never want to do this again.* (It would not be the last time I was on this detail, however. I found myself in trouble with the platoon sergeant on more than one occasion.) Come to find out, other units on the hill also had to supply details for the horrible, smelly work that had to be done, so we wouldn't have to do all of them. We cleaned four latrines that morning, and I want to tell you, I was tired, smelly, and not in a good mood when I returned to my squad around lunch time. The guys laughed at me again and told me they had done that detail many times themselves and I would get used to it. I started to go to chow with them, but they told me, "Hell no. Shower, shave, and put on a clean uniform before you leave for chow." After chow, I could get a few hours' sleep before heading out for the night ambush.

That's when I made my second mistake. I left for the shower and forgot my weapon. I didn't think I needed it in the shower.

As I walked along, I was stopped by an old, grizzled looking, mean man that turned out to be the regimental sergeant major. He scolded me for not having my weapon, took my name and unit, and told me to go get it. I did as I was told. When I finally got some lunch and returned to the tent, my squad leader was pissed. He told me the sergeant major had reported me to our company first sergeant, and he jumped all over him for not supervising me properly. Needless to say, I was on the shit burning detail once again the next day.

I was finally able to get some rest, but it seemed like I no sooner lay down when I was awakened and told to get my shit together for the night ambush. Mike told me all the gear I would need and said we would be in soft covers that night, not helmets. As luck would have it, Mike and Dave hid my soft cover so when I showed for inspection, I had my helmet on. Bill immediately jumped me about being out of uniform again, but Mike and Dave fessed up to messing with me one more time and produced my soft cover. Bill told Mike and Dave to leave me alone from now on, and they did.

MY FIRST NIGHT AMBUSH

Right about the time it started to get dark, we departed the perimeter. We went down the hill, and across the bridge—locked and loaded. I was forth in the line of march. Bill put me between Mike and another guy and was told to watch me. I thought, *This ain't too bad*, but it wasn't dark yet.

We skirted a village and we could see the villagers settling in for the night. They knew it wasn't a good idea to be wandering around at night there because anyone moving at night was considered the enemy. The enemy owned the night, as I would soon discover. We moved into some dense vegetation and it suddenly got dark real quick. I could no longer see the man in front of me, and that scared the hell out of me. I moved close and ran right into him. He was only two steps ahead of me. I could have reached out and touched him, but it was so dark, I couldn't tell how far away he was.

He said something like, "Back the hell up," and we continued.

I tried not to make any noise, but it was nearly impossible. Thank God everyone else was making noise, too. We traveled for what seemed like days, but in reality it was only for about two hours. We had reached our ambush site. We were supposed to be set up off of a trail junction, but I couldn't see a thing. Mike came up from behind me and told me which way to point my weapon. He said he would be right beside me and to settle in for the night. I lay down on my stomach very carefully and tried to get comfortable. Unfortunately, I had not adjusted my equipment for lying down and, of course, was lying right on one of my canteens. I tried to readjust, but it only made it worse. Mike whispered for me to be quiet and quit moving. I lay there for a long time, scared, uncomfortable, and unable to move.

We were there most of the night. That was the longest night ever. It seemed like we lay there for a week. Sometime around 0100 hours, I heard rustling from my left. Mike scooted over next to me and whispered that there was movement coming down the trail. He told me not to shoot until someone else shot first. All of a sudden, all hell broke loose. Our M60 was spitting out rounds so fast it made me lose my hearing for a moment. I opened up on semi-automatic with my M14, not wanting to waste ammo. I had only brought six magazines with me so I wouldn't have to carry that ammo can. I did have extra ammo in small boxes, though. I could not see what I was shooting at, but I figured I must be hitting something. I fired two magazines and had loaded the third when everyone stopped firing. It seemed like we were firing for a long time, but it was only a minute or two. As we lay there, I wondered what we were firing at, or if we hit anything. Mike scooted over to me and told me we would move back about a hundred meters or so into the jungle and wait until morning, then go back and check the ambush site. I was really nervous, and my adrenaline was pumping. All I was thinking was: I have two empty magazines.

I decided I would try to reload them in the dark. Of course when you load a magazine, each round makes a clicking sound when you shove the bullet into the magazine. The sound it made at night was magnified twice as loud as during the day. The squad leader told me to knock it off. We moved out about five minutes later. Again, I couldn't see a thing and kept wondering how the hell Bill knew where we were going. We got to our next position and waited. Just before sunrise, we got up and moved out again. It was a little chilly that morning and fog had started to roll in. We moved back to the ambush site. We got down where we were the night before and I could finally see the trail. It was only a few feet from where I was lying. We were told to watch real close; Bill and Dave were going to check the trail. They crawled out of position and moved out. They were gone about five minutes. They returned and told us to get up, that we were moving back to the hill. It only took us about an hour to get back. We were closer than I thought.

We had not moved in a straight line that night to get to the site, but dog-legged our movement. When we got back, I was exhausted. Before we could go to chow, our platoon sergeant and platoon commander came to the tent to debrief us. Bill gave him the highlights and said he saw several blood trails at the ambush site, but no bodies. We had hit something, but no confirmed kills. Bill then said something that disturbed the hell out of me. He told the lieutenant that I was a walking cluster fuck, and he wanted me out of his squad. He was pissed at me. I guess I just didn't fit in. I was hurt deeply. I didn't know the guy hated me so bad. I had to answer my own questions that day. Was I that bad, and was I going to make it another twelve and a half months?

We were excused and told to go to chow and get cleaned up. The lieutenant (LT) told me to report to him after chow. I really let myself down. I thought to myself, *Well, you did it again.* Other than making too much noise at the ambush site, I thought I had done pretty good for my first night ambush. Mike and Dave tried to reassure me while we ate chow that I didn't do that bad, and not to worry about it. Easy for them to say.

I reported to the LT after chow as told. He and the platoon sergeant were drinking coffee and going over an upcoming operation. I knocked and they told me to enter.

I stood at attention as was taught, and said in a loud voice, "Sir, PFC Tackett, reporting as ordered, sir."

He told me to relax and to sit down. He said for some reason Bill just didn't like me, and I would not be going back to Bill's squad. Bill had been in country a long time, was about to go home, and didn't have time for a cherry in his squad. Third squad would be back later that day from Da Nang, and I would be joining them. He then told me to go take a shower and get some rest. The shower and rest would not come. The platoon sergeant stopped me outside the tent and told me to report to the shit burning detail. No problem, I had done that now for two days in a row. No rest again.

CHAPTER 7

THIRD SQUAD:

THE WILD BUNCH

We are surrounded. That simplifies the problem.

– Chesty Puller, USMC

I don't know why I called them the wild bunch. I guess it's because the first time I saw them, they seemed like the most motley crew I had ever seen. It scared me more than I already was. Without knowing them and knowing what they were suspected of doing, I had no idea what I was about to get myself into.

About noon, I had completed my shit burning detail. I went back to first squad tent to collect my gear when I saw a crusty looking sergeant talking to Bill. They both looked at me when I came in, and Bill said, "There's your shit bird now." It was obvious I was the shit bird. I stood at attention and started to introduce myself. My new squad leader's name was Frank Powers. He looked as tough as nails. I was once again scared to death. I knew they were talking about me, and that wasn't good. I figured my goose was cooked.

Frank said, "Tack, get your gear and go to the next tent and settle in."

He called me Tack. To this day, he still calls me Tack. I didn't even know he knew my name. He then told me to get a shower and some chow and he would talk to me later.

I said, "Yes, sergeant," and started to walk out.

He then said, "That will be enough of that "sergeant" shit. My name is Frank." I had never called a sergeant by his first name before, but I said okay, and left.

As I walked into the next tent, there were about five guys standing around. They didn't look happy, so I figured I'd just find a rack, stow my gear, and head off to the showers. A guy with no shirt on came over to me and introduced himself as Marvin. He was from Washington state. He said he was a lance corporal and my new team leader. He welcomed me to third squad and told me he had already been told of my latest escapades with first squad. I just hung my head. He told me not to worry about it and that they were a bunch of ass holes. He then told me to get cleaned up, go to chow. And we, of course, had hole watch that night.

I did as I was told and met up with Frank later on that afternoon. He told me to go to the headquarters tent and find a guy named Trucker. Trucker would have some extra canteens for me. Trucker's real name was Rich, but I didn't find that out until many years later. He was headed home and was in third squad. I think I was his replacement. I met Trucker, got the extra gear and talked to him for a while. He said the squad was the best in the battalion. I figure everyone said that about their squad, but it was still reassuring. He said third squad was always tapped for the recon missions because Frank was a master of reconnaissance. Frank felt at home in the bush and would rather be out in the bush than in the rear, where he always seemed to find trouble. I would feel right at home there because I had been in trouble since I got there.

He told me Frank had been busted in rank, promoted, busted again, and promoted again. He just wouldn't take crap from anyone. He was also a fighter and would fight at a drop of a hat. He knew how to take care of his squad and would kill for them, especially with what had just happened with the investigation in Da Nang. I asked Trucker how he got his name. He explained that his MOS was truck driver, but when he got to the battalion, they needed grunts. He spent his entire tour in third squad as a grunt and never drove a truck. That's why they called him Trucker.

I didn't see Trucker again until 2001, when I attended my first Kilo 3/7 reunion in Tucson, Arizona. I didn't recognize anyone until finally a guy came up to me and said he knew me. It was Trucker. Of course, I had no idea who he was because he introduced himself as Rich. It was only after some discussion that I figured out it was Trucker from many years earlier. He had remembered me. Rich had a memory like a steel trap. He seemed to know everyone. Rich became one of my best friends and would call me at least once a week. Rich died in 2010 of cancer related to Agent Orange. Welcome home, Rich.

I returned to our squad's tent, with Frank starting to brief the squad on the night's hole watch mission. He introduced me to the squad as Tack. The squad wasn't in a talking mood and continued their preparation for night operations. Marvin came over to ensure I had everything I needed. The first thing Marvin told me was I had to get rid of the damn ammo can I used to carry my M14 magazines in. He had to think of what to use since there was no ammo pouches available. They were issuing the new M16 rifle and the magazines were smaller, and the M14 magazine wouldn't fit in the M16 ammo pouch. He came up with a brilliant idea. He took a canvas bag that carried M203 rounds, emptied the rounds, and had me put my magazines in it. It worked perfectly. I only had to put one of my pairs of socks in it to keep them from rattling around and making too much noise. Problem solved. Marvin did what Clint Eastwood would say years later in a movie, "Marines are trained to improvise, adapt, and overcome."

We went to chow, attended guard mount, and prepared for another sleepless night in a bunker. I was with Marvin and a guy named Ricky Lopez from Texas. Marvin was a quiet guy, didn't have much to say about anything. He told me just to watch him, Ricky, and the other guys in the squad and I'd be okay. I was glad I was in third squad; it took a lot of pressure off, at least for a while.

The night went off without incident. The next morning, we were relieved and sent to chow and to get some sleep. After chow, everyone was settling in for a nap. I started to get my cover and head out when Frank asked me where I was going. I told him I had the shit burning detail and the platoon sergeant would be looking for me. He said, "That shit stops now." He told me to take a nap; he would square things away with the platoon sergeant. I did as I was told, grateful for a couple of hours of sleep. I slept right up until lunch. Marvin woke me and told me to get some chow. By now, I was aware of the routine. I got my uniform straight, brushed off my boots, grabbed my rifle and cover, and went to chow. What could go wrong? As I was walking to chow, I noticed Bill and another Marine I didn't know coming towards me.

Bill yelled, "Hey shit bird!"

I responded with the most evil look I could muster, but said nothing. Bill didn't like the look I gave him and came over to confront me. I stood my ground, but Bill was on a mission to destroy me for some reason.

About that time, Frank appeared and got between me and Bill and told Bill to back off saying, "It ends now. You screw with Tack again, you screw with me. Let it be."

I never had another problem with Bill. I saw Bill at the reunion in Tucson, also. He didn't remember any of what went on and barely remembered me. He also told me he wiped out most of his memory of those times with drugs and alcohol, but he was good to go now. He had been clean and sober for over thirty years. He apologized for everything, and we had a good laugh.

I was still concerned the squad would be looking at me as a CID agent, so I decided to talk to Marvin about it. Marvin explained all the FNG's were not always accepted immediately in the squad and I would have to earn their trust. It would all come down to how I reacted when the shit hit the fan.

Later that day, the entire platoon had a briefing by the platoon commander. This was the first time I was with the whole platoon. These guys looked salty. He explained we would be departing Hill 55 on a two week mission to recover some sort of printing press used by the Viet Cong to print and distribute propaganda about Americans. We would depart as a company in two days. He gave the squad leaders the packing list of what to take and we broke up and went back to our tents. Frank explained we didn't have hole watch that night, which would be my first night I had some time off since I arrived in Vietnam. I finally got to write my first letters home and give my girlfriend and family my new address.

Marines live for their mail. We didn't have fancy cell phones or computers then. All we had was mail. They told me it would take about a week for my mail to reach home and about a week to ten days for their mail to reach me. It all depended on where we were at the time the mail was delivered. They attempted to get mail to us in the field when we were out on operations, but most of the time we would have to wait until we returned. It would be almost a month before I got any mail.

The next day, we were issued all our ammo, hand grenades, light anti-tank weapons (LAWs), smoke grenades, C-rations, and extra socks, which was a surprise. We were loaded for bear. I had not carried this much equipment to date and didn't know if I would be able to take it or not. This was my first combat action with third squad and I did not want to fail. There were seven of us in our squad. The organization of a squad usually consisted of eleven, but we never had more than seven or eight. Guys would get wounded, killed, or rotate home. That's just the way it was. Marvin inspected my gear and helped me get squared away. Finally, the day would come when I would be tested under fire in the bush. I would find out it would be much different than the ambush on the truck on the way to Hill 55.

The morning we were to depart, the lieutenant came into our tent. We were squaring it away for the next group of grunts to come in. We would not be returning to Hill 55 because the end of the operation would take us back to Hill 37. I was happy to hear that; I liked it there. The LT called the squad together and said the CID investigation had been completed, there was no evidence that third squad had committed the offenses. The local Vietnamese swore it was Americans that murdered the girl, but the evidence did not support their claim. The squad was relieved and could get back to the business of the day. It seemed like a big weight was lifted from their shoulders. They became more outgoing with me which made me feel right at home. The mood lightened tremendously.

As we moved out, our platoon was in the lead. When the company formed up, it seemed like there must have been a hundred of us. In fact, the real number was probably more like seventy-five to eighty—as I said before, we were never at full strength. Third squad was second in the line of march, and we headed out to the unknown. We moved for about four hours. We started out going through a village, then to open rice patties, which made everyone nervous, then finally into the bush. It seemed like easy travel for a while, but we weren't up front breaking brush. You never traveled on trails unless it couldn't be helped. The lead squad was getting their asses kicked from the thick brush, so we switched. We were in the lead. I was the third guy from the point man.

It was tough working our way through the underbrush. We got deeper into the jungle, and it only got thicker. The point man, Ricky, was really being careful not to hit any booby traps or mines. I learned a lot just watching him move methodically through the brush, his weapon in one hand and a machete in the other. We finally took a break sometime around noon. It was hot and humid and sweat was rolling off all of us. We formed a small perimeter and broke out some C-rations to eat. I had already gone through two canteens of water so Marvin told me I had better not drink it all because we would not get a resupply until sometime the next day. We moved out again, this time moving to the rear of the platoon. It was someone else's turn to break brush. We must have moved for another two or three hours when the word came down to form a platoon perimeter. We would be here overnight. Frank came around and placed Ricky and me in a position together. We were to watch the trail we had come upon. One of us would start to dig in for the night while the other watched the trail. It started to get dark, and everyone settled in. It was going to be another very dark night. Even though I was right next to Ricky, I could not see him.

We were told we were to do 50 percent watch. That meant one guy sleeps, while one watches. Watch what? I couldn't see a thing. Ricky told me to listen; I wouldn't be able to see a thing and that's why it was important to learn the jungle sounds. About an hour into my watch, I started hearing movement in the trees. My imagination was running wild.

Suddenly, somewhere from up in the trees, someone started yelling, "Fuck you, fuck you!"

I couldn't believe what I was hearing. This guy had some nerve. He was one ballsy VC. I woke Ricky and told him what was going on and asked if I should shoot up in the trees. He laughed at me and told me it was a lizard. I thought he was joking, but he said, "No, they call it a fuck you lizard because the noise it makes sounds just like fuck you." I was on my toes for my watch and couldn't sleep, so I took Ricky's first hour of watch. I finally woke him and told him what I had done. He would not return the favor. In two hours, he woke me and I was on watch again. He told me I needed to take every advantage to rest, even if I couldn't sleep. Another lesson learned.

Early the next morning, I made my first big mistake in the field. It was a mistake I would take to heart because it could have gotten other Marines and me killed. Just as it started to get light, we were all put on alert. I was told that was the time the enemy liked to attack because everyone would be sleepy or just waking up and not as alert. I was watching down the trail, Ricky was preparing a cup of C-ration coffee and his breakfast. Ricky had his back up against a tree and couldn't see down the trail. I was on watch while he fixed and ate his breakfast; then it would be my turn. It was just getting where I could actually see down the trail, and there was still a mist in the air from the humidity. As I watched, all of a sudden, I saw a lone Viet Cong soldier walking down the trail right at us. He didn't seem to have a care in the world. His AK47 rifle was slung over his shoulder, and he had a small bag hanging from his belt. He was wearing the black pajamas I had heard so much about and a conical hat they all wore. This was the second enemy soldier I had ever seen. The first was the one that died on the LZ when I first got there. I had only been in country about three weeks now and was about to get my first kill.

Instead of doing as I was trained, (move slowly, raise my rifle, take careful aim, then shoot a single round, which would have been an easy shot because he was so close) I grabbed my rifle, flipped it on automatic, and cut loose with an entire magazine of eighteen rounds of ammo. It happened so fast that I didn't take time to think. My shots went wild into the trees breaking the silence of the morning.

I could hear everyone hollering at me, trying to figure out what was going on. Ricky hit the deck spilling his coffee everywhere. Then I did the unthinkable. I jumped up out of the hole and ran down the trail after the guy. Of course, I didn't hit him even though he was only about twenty yards away, but I was not going to let him get away. I didn't grab my gear, just my weapon. I also forgot to reload another magazine in the weapon so my weapon was empty. Ricky was yelling at me to come back, but I wasn't listening. I wanted my kill.

When I got to where the VC was, the only thing there was his conical hat lying on the ground. There were no blood trails or anything. I didn't hit a damn thing. I stood there for a second when Ricky came up beside me and told me to get my ass back to the hole. It was then that I realized I had made a huge mistake. We carefully moved back to the hole with Ricky telling me to go first as he covered our movement. When we got back, Frank, Marvin the LT, and our platoon sergeant were standing there. The entire platoon was on high alert by now, and the company commander was asking for a sit rep on the radio. The LT told him to stand by, and he asked me what happened. When I tried to explain, it hit me like a ton of bricks. I had made the biggest mistake a grunt could make.

You see, sometimes the enemy wants you to chase him so you can lead your squad into an ambush. If that happens, you and the other Marines will most likely be killed. The platoon sergeant was just shaking his head. The LT told Frank to square my ass away, and we would handle it when we got to the rear. He left talking to the commanding officer (CO) on the radio. Frank and Marvin were looking at me in disbelief. Frank told Marvin and Ricky to explain to me what I had done wrong and that it had better never happen again or he would shoot me himself. I couldn't tell if Frank meant it or not—at the time, I'm sure he did.

I stood there in amazement at the huge mistake I had made, when I looked down and saw that I had picked up the conical hat. It was my first war trophy. I held it up to show Ricky, but all he said was, "Fucking cherry" and a bunch of stuff in Spanish which I didn't understand but knew probably wasn't good. I had disappointed my squad already and only two days in the bush.

For punishment for my bad decision, I was put on point. Our movement did become easier. We were in double and triple canopy jungle and the undergrowth wasn't so bad. I moved very carefully, sometimes too slowly because I was told to move a little faster. I did not want to repeat the mistake of the morning and didn't want to get killed either. We moved until we reached a large creek. The water was clear and cold. I didn't realize it, but we had entered the Que Son mountain range. It didn't seem like we were moving up hill, but we had been for almost two hours. I stopped at the edge of the creek, got down (as I was trained), and gave the hand and arm signal to Ricky that I had come upon a danger area. A danger area is described as an open area with concealment on one or more sides that could be hiding an ambush. Frank came forward and told me to stand by.

The LT came up and said we were to cross the creek, which now seemed more like a small river, and secure the other side. Ricky and I were told to move as quietly as possible through the water to the other side. We lowered ourselves down the bank and into the water which was about waist deep and cold. It felt good because we were sweaty and hot. This would be the time we would be most vulnerable to enemy fire. The creek was about twenty to thirty feet across and stayed about waist high, but we got to the other side without a problem. Ricky and I secured it by making sweeping moves in a circle to make sure nobody was watching. Ricky gave Frank the hand signal that all was secure, and the rest of the platoon crossed. We formed our perimeter and waited for instructions.

It was decided we would remain there the rest of the day and that the other two platoons would cross in other areas to do small squad patrols to check the area out. We decided to fill our canteens at the creek since we would be there awhile. It was a welcome break. Ricky gathered up all the empty canteens, secured them to his belt, and told me to guard him at the edge of the creek while he filled them. I was glad we filled our canteens because by now, I was down to less than one canteen of water. We were told we would not be getting a resupply that day because a helicopter could not land anywhere around where we were. We filled our squad's canteens and went back to the perimeter. I know I was taught not to drink the water, but it looked clear, clean, and was cold. I started to take a drink when Marvin stopped me. He said we had to use our iodine tablets first. We would have to put two tablets in each canteen and wait at least an hour before we could drink it. The iodine tablets would kill any parasites and germs in the water. It would make the water taste really bad, but it could save you from a lifetime of dysentery or any other number of bad stomach diseases.

We remained there for the rest of the day. That evening, while eating our C-rations, I asked Ricky if Frank was really that mad at me for what I had done that morning. Ricky said I had done something stupid, but Frank would forget about it as long as I didn't make the same mistake again. Frank was good like that. I was relieved at that, but the platoon sergeant wasn't as forgiving.

It was decided we would stay in that area for a couple of days. We were to do squad patrols out in different directions to try to find a good LZ for resupply and medevac if needed. We patrolled for a couple of days without incident. Another platoon did find a suitable LZ. There didn't seem to be any sign of the enemy anywhere. The only sign of the enemy was the one I saw the first day. I guess they figured he went and told all his buddies, and they high tailed it out of the area. I was getting pretty comfortable now with the squad, but they still did not let me forget my big mistake. Finally, we were told we would be moving back to Hill 37. Another platoon had found the printing press. It was old, rusty, and had not been used in years. It was hidden in a thicket that used to be a VC headquarters. The little village had long been abandoned years before and was all overgrown. The printing press could not be used again because of all the rust on it.

We followed the creek out of the mountains for the next couple of days without incident. Finally, we could see Hill 37 off in the distance and only had to cross the open area of rice paddies leading back to the hill. I was still on point for our platoon, and Ricky told me to be really careful on the rice paddy dike because the VC knew we had to travel on them. The rice paddies were filled with water and they would sometimes booby trap the dike. By now, I had worn the same set of jungle utilities for the last ten days. I would only change socks and t-shirts. My utility trousers were cut and shredded, and I must have smelled like the shitters that I had burned. I guess I didn't notice how bad I smelled because every one of us smelled the same.

We got across the rice paddy and entered the village of Dai Loc, just below Hill 37. Little kids (which we called "slicky boys" because they could steal us blind and we wouldn't even notice) gathered around us trying to sell us cold cokes and their sisters. I was trying to be friendly with them, but I was told to leave them alone. We entered the perimeter like returning conquering heroes. I had my conical hat strapped to my butt pack, and as we walked towards the company area, the rear echelon mother fuckers (REMFs) watched. They almost looked envious. I had made it through my first operation almost without incident, almost.

We formed up in front of the company tent and the company commander came out. He had gotten back earlier with another platoon. He made a short speech about how well we did, that we had taken no casualties, and had accomplished our mission. We were told we would be on stand down for a week. Stand down was time when we got our stuff together: cleaned equipment and uniforms, rested, went to the corpsman if we needed medical attention, and ate hot chow again. We were told to secure, but our platoon was on the quick reaction force (QRF)—a force used in an emergency if another unit got in trouble and needed assistance.

It was about noon when we got back to the squad tent, so Frank told us to put our gear in the tent and head to chow. It would be our first real hot meal in more than ten days, so we were anxious to get there. The entire squad went together, and Frank told me when I got my tray of food to come and eat with Marvin and him—he wanted to talk to me. I was nervous because I knew what it was about. When we got in the chow line, we were filthy, smelly, and looking like crap. About that time, one or two of our guys from the platoon had entered the chow tent. The mess sergeant came out and said we weren't coming in his mess tent until we got cleaned up. An argument started with a lot of swearing and name calling. Frank started to go to the head of the line to straighten this guy out when out of nowhere, appeared our LT. He got right up in the mess sergeant's face and told him his men were going inside to eat, and if he had a problem with that to take it up with the battalion executive officer (XO, normally a major). Apparently, this mess sergeant hadn't been in country too long, and this was his first and last attempt to turn someone away from his mess tent. I heard Ricky say he was glad the LT was there because Frank would have cut the mess sergeant's throat.

I got my food, and it actually smelled good. The only thing was they had that damn green Kool-Aid again. I did manage to get some cold milk, though, and I then went and sat with Frank, Marvin, and Ricky. Frank told me that I had made a huge error in judgment that first morning in the bush, but I had learned a good lesson and that I did very well the rest of the operation. The only thing was the platoon sergeant hadn't forgotten about it. I was to report to the platoon sergeant for, you guessed it, shit burning detail. I ate, didn't even go to clean up, and reported for shit burning detail. Apparently, I hadn't been the only one out there that had screwed up, because there were three other guys I'd never met, just as nasty looking as me, ready to burn crap. 364 days and a wake-up.

Pvt. Donald D. Tackett's friend Rich
Vietnam 1967

Pvt. Donald D. Tackett's friend Rich
Philadelphia 2008

Frank 1968   Pvt. Donald G. Tackett
Note the Conical Hat above my head.
First war souvenir

Frank and Marvin   First trip down Liberty Road and
First ambush
December 1967

Pvt. Donald G. Tackett
Hill 37, 1967

CHAPTER 8
THE DEADLIEST NIGHT

Sometimes it's entirely appropriate to kill a fly with sledgehammer.

– MAJ Holdridge, USMC

It was funny to me, and only me, that the only shots fired on the previous week's operation were fired by me, an FNG. In terms of combat operations, it was considered a walk in the park. I guess the fact I had retrieved the conical hat saved my ass, because had I not gotten it, nobody would have ever believed an FNG had even seen a VC or that one ever existed.

The next morning after chow, I found out I didn't have the shit burning detail. The platoon was exchanging equipment, so I decided to go to supply and see if I could get some new jungle utilities. My trousers were shredded, and I didn't have enough thread in my sewing kit to repair them. I took my war souvenir with me to show PFC Bock in the orderly room. I went in, and he told me we should go outside to talk, I could show him my conical hat out there. He confirmed what I had expected. I had been branded as a shit bird. He said that, had I not gotten the conical hat, I would have been in real trouble. I would have probably had to stand before the company commander in Captain's Mass, a form of non-judicial punishment, or at least gotten a written reprimand. I had given away the company's position and had probably compromised the entire operation.

Bock said the gook that got away more than likely did go back to where he came from and tell his buddies and they'd "di di'd" (Vietnamese for left or departed) out of the area. He did say the commander thought it might have saved lives. However, we wouldn't be able to set up another ambush later, since we knew they were there. Who really knows how my actions affected the operation? All we knew was nobody was wounded or killed.

I asked Bock what happened to shit birds like me. He said the worst thing that could happen was I would be sent to a Civil Action Platoon (CAP), or Civil Action Group (CAG). Either way they were both bad. Those battalions get requirements every now and then to provide grunts for duty, and most of the time they send the shit birds. I asked what a CAP or CAG was.

He explained it was a squad of Marines that lives, eats, and fights with a platoon or company of South Vietnamese Regulars (ARVNs), or Popular Forces units (PFs). It's horrible duty and the life expectancy of a grunt there was only measured by the next time that unit was hit. The PFs and ARVNs, as they were called, had a tendency to disappear during a battle. They left the Marines to do all the fighting and just cut out. The ARVN's and PF's were only out to protect their family and nothing else. That worried me without a doubt. Bock said there hadn't been a requirement sent down in a long time, and it was about time they should get one. There were several CAP units around Hill 37 and Hill 55. They hadn't seen much action lately, so that's why there hadn't been a need for any replacements in a while. He knew one kid that only lasted two days there before he was killed. I left Bock sensing my time in Kilo was limited. I had sealed my own fate already with the platoon sergeant, and there was no doubt in my mind I would be the next to go. Bock did assure me of one thing. Most of the time they sent the guys that had been caught with drugs first and had been to Captain's Mass or Office Hours before, another form of non-judicial punishment.

I went ahead to the supply tent to try to exchange my trousers. The supply sergeant was there and had the new camouflage jungle fatigues. He went ahead and gave me two new sets. I was excited. Everyone else was still wearing the olive green jungle fatigues. When I got back to the tent, Marvin asked me where I got the camo's. I explained what I had done. He advised me not to wear them because nobody else had them, and I would fall out of favor with the squad if I wore the new camos. I decided to put them away and just wear my old stuff. It was definitely a good decision.

When we went to chow that evening, all the REMF's in the rear were wearing the new camo. None of the grunts had been given any yet. Grunts always got stuff last. That made for a bad situation. All the grunts in the mess tent started hassling the REMF's, and all hell broke loose. Trays started flying, food was everywhere—it was almost a riot. About that time, the idiot mess sergeant came out from the kitchen to see what was going on. And wouldn't you know it, he had the new camo uniform on, too. That just made a bad situation worse. Finally, a few senior NCO's got everyone separated, and as fast as the fight got started, it ended. Someone saw the battalion commander and XO coming to eat and hollered that they were on their way, so the mess tent emptied very quickly. I had just gotten my tray and was hungry, so I sat down to eat. The battalion commander came in, saw the mess, and was pissed. He yelled for the mess sergeant, who by now had retreated back to the kitchen, and demanded an explanation.

When the mess sergeant told him what had happened, the commander grabbed the battalion XO and told him to have everyone in the rear turn in the camos and get them issued to the grunts first, and that had better be the last time the grunts got the new equipment last. He looked at me; by now I was standing at attention. He told me to be at ease and continue eating. He instructed the mess sergeant to get a detail and get the mess tent squared away. The mess sergeant looked at me as if to say "come help me," but he decided against it and went back to the kitchen. I'm glad he didn't tell me to help because I would have probably told him no and been in more trouble. I finished eating as fast as I could and got the hell out of there.

The next couple of days were uneventful. We practiced movement techniques, immediate action drills, and had some map reading classes, as well as communications classes. Frank told me he was going to make me his radio telephone operator (RTO) as soon as the old RTO rotated back to the states in a month or so. I started learning all about the heavy PRC 25 radio I was about to carry. I read the communications electronic operating instruction (CEOI) manual, a book that tells you encoding and decoding procedures for messages as well as the frequencies we operated on. It was a complicated system, but vital to everyday operations in the unit.

The day came when I finally got mail. I had been in country now for about five weeks and was wondering if I was ever going to see any mail. I got a letter from my mom and two from my girlfriend. I also got a package from my uncle, who had served in the Korean War. The package was filled with all sorts of goodies and a short note. He said he would have Mr. Zakney, from Zakney's grocery store, box me up a goody box once a month and send it. That was great. In the box was a bleach bottle with the lid taped tightly on. I couldn't figure out why the hell my uncle was sending me bleach. I cut the tape on the lid and opened it. It was filled with whiskey. He had cleaned out the bleach bottle real good and filled it up with liquor. What a surprise. I guess he figured we couldn't get alcohol in Vietnam and sent me some. What was funny was that I had never drank liquor before, just beer. I didn't like the taste of it, so I shared it with the squad—who had no trouble disposing of it. The entire time I was there, my uncle sent me a total of eleven packages. I actually only received six. Nobody could ever explain what happened to the other five, but I figured it was most likely pilfered somewhere along the line, probably by the REMF's in the rear area.

We had only been alerted a couple of times for the QRF mission. The first was during the day, when a squad of Marines was escorting the battalion surgeon and dentist down to the village of Dai Loc below the hill to do some medical and dental work for the villagers. I couldn't understand why they would send the dentist because the older women in the village would chew this stuff called beetle nut, which turned their teeth completely black. The squad was ambushed, which was strange because they were ambushed close to the hill and during the middle of the day, too. By the time we reacted and reached the squad, everything was over. There were no injuries, just two scared doctors.

The other incident was when India Company had run into a large North Vietnamese force, so the entire Kilo company was put on alert, and we had to stand by the LZ to be air lifted to their location to help. That incident also ended quickly, so we were released before we even left the hill.

Somewhere around midnight, two days before we were relieved, our platoon was alerted for QRF. A squad of Marines assigned to a CAP unit and guarding a bridge had been hit and overrun. We were to muster quickly, jump on the awaiting AMTRACS (a large track vehicle capable of carrying a lot of Marines), and head out. The squad that was hit had been guarding a small bridge that crossed a river that led to the village an ARVN unit was living in. There was a squad of Marines and a squad of ARVNs guarding the bridge that night. When we were riding down the road on top of the AMTRAC, we could see tracers flying everywhere ahead of us. The battle was still going on. Our LT had the AMTRACs stop there, and we proceeded on foot straight down the road, something we didn't do often, but these guys were in trouble, and we had to move fast.

Our squad was in the lead, it was dark, but we could see pretty good. The artillery was firing illumination rounds and they lit up the night. We moved slowly on the side of the road until we reached the first bunker by the bridge. We couldn't see inside the bunker, but we secured both sides of it. The firing had stopped by now, and we could smell the cordite in the air from all the firing and hand grenade explosions. Frank got out his flashlight and lit up the inside of the bunker. There were two Marines in there badly wounded. He jumped in, and I jumped in behind him. The rest of the platoon came up and crossed the bridge very carefully to the other bunker on the far side of the bridge. Frank called for the corpsman to come up. I got out of the bunker as the corpsman entered. Both Marines were still alive, but severely wounded. As the Doc did his thing, we continued to scan the jungle to the right and left. Frank came out of the bunker and said one Marine had died, but the other was still alive. He said the Marine told him the ARVNs had split, leaving them there to defend the bridge themselves. Frank was pissed. He said there were still two Marines missing from the bunker, and the one live Marine did not know what had happened to them.

The LT told Frank to take three guys and sweep the tree line to try to locate the other two Marines. The LT told us the four Marines on the other side of the bridge were all dead. The LT had sent the other two squads out on the other side of the bridge to try to locate the two missing Marines there. Frank, Marvin, Ricky, and I went out. We moved slowly and quietly. I was not as scared as I had been on previous operations but was scared enough to be alert. We got about a hundred meters into the jungle when we heard moaning. Frank told us to stay put, and he crawled to where the moaning was coming from. He found one of the Marines. He was wounded, but would be okay.

He said the VC had captured them and took them into the jungle. He was able to fight them off. He killed the one that had been watching him, but he was shot by another while trying to escape. That was about the time we showed up. They had taken off, dragging the other Marine with them. We heard the shot and feared the worse. We took the wounded Marine back to the bridge, and Frank asked the LT if he could take our squad out to find the other Marine. The LT said to go out no more than 300 meters, loop around, and return. We were not to go far because they could be waiting to ambush us.

We went back to where we found the wounded Marine and continued on. This time Ricky was on point and Frank was right behind him. I was behind him and his RTO. Ricky moved slowly and deliberately looking for signs of the missing Marine. He came upon the VC the wounded Marine had killed. About an hour later, we returned to the bridge not having any luck finding the missing man. It was starting to get light. The wounded had been evacuated by the AMTRACs back to Hill 37. The dead were being bagged and tagged. It was when it got light that I saw how desperately these Marines had fought. There were empty rifle casings everywhere. All M16 and M60 casings. The ARVNs didn't fire a round. The Marines had their bayonets attached to their weapons, which meant they were in hand to hand combat. There was blood everywhere.

I could see in Frank's eyes that he was getting madder and madder. He started cussing and throwing things all around the area. He said we were going to go into the village and kill every one of the chicken shit ARVNs. The LT and platoon sergeant came over to settle him down. I knew there was nothing I could do to help him. I was also pissed. I had seen my first dead Marine. I helped put two of them in body bags after the corpsman finished attaching the casualty tags. I would be changed forever. I just wanted to kill something. If Frank had told us to go into the village and kill anything that walked, we probably would have. I had never felt anger like that in my life. I had carried dead Marines in body bags before, but had never seen them outside. I had let myself believe I was only carrying a heavy bag. This time it was different. I saw their faces. One Marine's eyes were open. He was just staring out into space. He was no longer in pain. He had been shot several times in the torso. We could see he had put up a fight by all the blood around him.

The LT had us police up the area for equipment and scoop up all the empty ammo casings. We would not leave anything behind that the enemy could use. He even had us throw dirt over the blood to make any evidence of a fight disappear. Just about the time we were to move out and go back to the hill, a squad of ARVNs came out of the village. I thought Frank was going to lose it. Suddenly, he pointed his M16 at them and started cussing and yelling and calling them all sorts of names. Then he lifted his M16 in the air and fired off an entire magazine of ammo above their heads. They hit the ground and a couple of them got up and ran back into the village. The LT came running over and grabbed Frank. He then told him to move our squad out. We would walk back to Hill 37. The remainder of the platoon would stay there and wait for transportation to pick up the dead and secure the bridge until the ARVNs returned. It was heartbreaking to see those five body bags lined up on the road. I couldn't imagine what they had gone through the night before. What terror they must have experienced before their death. That could have been me, had I been sent to the CAP unit after I screwed up.

When we arrived back at the hill, we secured our gear and went to wash up before we went to breakfast. I saw Frank head out the back of the tent heading for the bunker line. I started to go after him, but Marvin told me to leave him alone, that he would be okay. He just needed to be alone. I didn't talk to Frank about it until later that night. He told me I had better get used to it.

"Did you ever get used to it?" I asked him

He said, "No, I guess you never will either."

The next day, I went to the orderly room and asked Bock if there were any the empty positions in the CAP units that had been overrun because I knew I had a chance to be transferred. He said no, that the battalion commander refused to fill the CAP unit with anymore Marines because of the lack of action by the ARVNs. He wasn't willing to lose Marines to that kind of duty when not one ARVN had been wounded or killed or even so much as fired a weapon. That was a huge relief to me. I was safe from going to a CAP unit for now.

We never knew if the missing Marine was ever found. Chances are, he died and was buried in the jungle by the enemy.

Shortly after, we were notified we would be coming off QRF to go back to regular missions. Our life of leisure was over. By now, everyone had been issued the new camo jungle fatigues, so I could finally wear mine. I was starting to look salty now. I was getting the tan lines everyone had, my hair was growing out from when I had it shaved before I came to Vietnam, and I was becoming more and more comfortable with the surroundings and the heat.

CHAPTER 9

TET, 1968

THE YEAR OF THE MONKEY

We could feel them moving all around us during the night.

— Unknown Marine, Khe Sanh

After the incident on the bridge, the battalion continued to send patrols out to attempt to recover the missing Marine. No sign of him ever turned up. During Operation Homecoming (when all the American POW's returned to the United States), to my knowledge, the missing Marine was not among them. His status remains Missing in Action.

It was right about this time that I figured I made the right decision back at Camp Pendleton at Staging Battalion. Remember when I said I had the decision to go to First Marine Division or Third Marine Division, and chose the First? Well, units of the Third Marine Division were stationed at a place called Khe Sanh, a remote Marine outpost on the farthest point north near the demilitarized zone. About the same time we had the incident on the bridge (21 January 1968), Khe Sanh was attacked by a sizable force of North Vietnamese soldiers, estimated around 40,000. Khe Sanh was surrounded and came under siege until around 6 April 1968. The NVA made many attempts to overrun the camp, but were turned back every time by the unit of Marines stationed on that hill. During the two and half month siege of Khe Sanh, 205 Americans lost their lives over seventy-seven days of fighting. That's the official number, but many say that number didn't take into account the ones that died as a result of their wounds afterwards. I found out that a Marine I went to basic training with lost his life at Khe Sanh.

I had definitely made the right decision.

With the attack on Khe Sanh going on, all units were placed on high alert. Our leaders knew something was about to happen, but no one expected what did.

The Vietnamese New Year was 31 January 1968, the year of the monkey. Tet is celebrated throughout Vietnam, and most of the ARVN units were on stand down so the soldiers could go home to celebrate. The North Vietnamese had also agreed to a cease fire so all of Vietnam could celebrate. Based on what was going on at Khe Sanh, nobody believed there would be a cease fire. What happened next was astonishing.

In early morning hours of 31 January 1968, the Viet Cong and North Vietnamese launched an attack on every major city and province in South Vietnam. The Viet Cong even managed to get inside the American Embassy in Saigon. Army military policemen fought them back, regaining the embassy. The Tet Offensive of 1968 had begun. This would prove to be the bloodiest part of the Vietnam war, with many Americans losing their lives, and many, many more Viet Cong and North Vietnamese losing theirs. Ho Chi Minh declared the Tet Offensive a great victory for the North. It would be the battle that changed the face of the war.

We continued our operations off of Hill 37 during that time. Things were relatively quiet because all the North Vietnamese and Viet Cong were concentrating their efforts on the big cities. There were many rumors that we were going to pack up and move to either Hue City or on north to Khe Sanh to help the besieged Third Marine Division. We remained on high alert. By now Frank had assigned me duty as his RTO. I knew I would be secure with the squad now and that I had earned Frank's trust. The RTO was always carrying the squad's communications equipment in the form of a PRC 25 radio, extra batteries, and personal equipment. That added about twenty-five pounds of weight to what I already carried. I was offered a .45 pistol, but decided to carry the M16 instead. I somehow felt safer with a rifle as opposed to a pistol.

In the second week of February, our squad was assigned a detail to provide security for an engineering unit that was trying to clear the roads heading up to Hue City. Road clearing details were always dangerous because we had to move slowly so the mine detectors could do their thing to make the roads safe for convoys for resupply. We were with an engineering unit and had two tanks along for protection. We were spread out on the road with the engineers in the front. Our squad was dispersed along the road, also. As the RTO, I was to stay as close to Frank as he would let me. I would pass on any radio traffic to him and hand him the hand set if he had to make a call for anything.

All of a sudden, we were ambushed by a large enemy force. One of the guys in our squad was wounded immediately in the initial shooting and was lying in the middle of the road. Everyone else dove for cover in a narrow ditch that ran alongside the road. Frank yelled for me to stay in the ditch and to call in a medevac helicopter. He got up and ran through the bullets hitting all around us to assist the wounded Marine. Frank started moving all around the road, positioning our squad to fire in the direction of the ambush. I had no idea what our position was, so I got up and ran after him. I remember the dirt flying up all around me from enemy rounds hitting near my feet as I ran. Frank pushed me behind one of the tanks and told me to stay put. Frank continued to expose himself to enemy fire while deploying the squad and helping the wounded Marine. He determined which direction the fire was coming from and directed all of our fire in that direction.

About that time, the engineer lieutenant came running up to Frank, hollering orders at him. Frank was still dealing with the wounded Marine, and now our corpsman was also wounded. The lieutenant continued to holler at Frank to move his men, when Frank grabbed him by the shirt and told him to get the fuck out of his way; he had everything under control. The lieutenant continued to yell and told Frank he was going to have him court marshaled. Frank then told him to get the hell out of there or he would shoot him. The LT left running back towards the front of the convoy.

Frank dragged the wounded Marine and the corpsman to safety and returned to the tank where I was with the radio. I had reached the battalion and informed them of the situation, but I didn't have our location. Frank grabbed the handset, called for the medevac, and then began calling for fire support. While all of this was happening, he grabbed the radio to the tank gunner and directed him where to fire his tank. He grabbed me, and we ran back to the ditch I was originally in. This time, he pointed to me and told me to stay there and keep my head down. Again, I could see bullets striking the dirt all around us. I don't know how they kept from hitting us. Frank took off again to continue the fight. I was shooting from the ditch, but I didn't know at what—I just fired into the brush alongside the road.

Because of Frank's quick reaction to the ambush, his expertise in deploying our squad and the engineers, and calling in for fire support, Frank was instrumental in forcing the enemy to break contact.

When we returned to the company, the commander wanted a debriefing from the squad. We were all in the commander's office when he said he didn't know whether to court martial Frank or give him a medal. The engineer lieutenant had made a formal complaint against Frank for insubordination and for making a death threat. The commander asked any of us if we had witnessed what the engineer lieutenant was talking about. Of course, I saw and heard the whole incident, but all of us said we didn't know what the LT was talking about and that Frank saved every one of our lives—including the engineers. Frank had controlled the entire situation from the time it started until the time it ended. The LT did nothing but run around and make a fool of himself.

The commander grinned and said he understood. The commander knew Frank's capabilities as a leader and also his temper. There was not a doubt in the commander's mind that Frank probably had threatened the LT, but it was okay by him. The wounded Marine and corpsman would survive because of Frank's actions, as well as our entire squad and all the engineers, including the dumb LT. Frank was submitted for an award of the Silver Star, our nation's third highest award for valor, for his actions that day. The entire squad was submitted for awards of the Bronze Star with "V" device. Frank would not receive his award until sometime later. His award was downgraded to a Bronze Star with "V" device. The "V" stands for Valor. Nobody else in the squad received an award; ours were not approved. Frank didn't know ours were not approved until many years later when I met him at the reunion in New Orleans. Frank was my hero that day and remains so. (Franks award citation can be read in Appendix A.)

The action in our area of operation started to increase after the first week of the Tet Offensive. The NVA and VC were attempting to exfiltrate out of the major cities back to sanctuaries in Cambodia and Laos. They were heading straight through our area of operation, called the Arizona Territory and Dodge City. The NVA and VC had skillfully infiltrated these areas prior to Tet, so they could launch their attacks on 31 January. The remaining units were now trying to get back. We were conducting many squad-size ambushes during this time, with carefully plotted artillery and mortar fire support in case we got in trouble.

One night, we were reconning along the river near Liberty Bridge. Frank decided we were going to hole up in a thicket near the riverbank for the night. We were on a small rise overlooking the river and a large trail. Since it was a recon mission, we were to avoid contact and only report movement of the enemy. If the opportunity came up, we could set up a hasty ambush, if the force we saw was small enough that we could handle it.

Around 2200 hours, I received a disturbing radio message. Normally during the night we would only use the radio to make commo checks by clicking the handset twice, and the rear area would click twice back, acknowledging our message. (There was absolutely no talking because sound carried in the jungle at night.) The message from the rear reported that a large enemy unit of heavily armed NVA were spotted heading straight towards our location. The message said it wasn't clear if it was an ARVN unit that was operating in that area or the enemy, but we were to remain on high alert.

It was finally confirmed it was a large North Vietnamese unit, not the ARVN's. They were about a thousand meters out and heading for us. Frank was given the option to try to move out or stay hidden in the thicket. Frank decided not to move because it would be too risky to move and we had the river to our back, which we could slip into to evade the enemy if necessary. We only had two other directions we could go: neither was a good option. We were well hidden, but there was still call for concern. Then Frank said what I had dreaded to hear since I got to Vietnam. He told us to fix bayonets. We were about to be in a world of shit. There was definitely a chance we would engage in hand to hand combat.

I was scared to death. All I could see in my mind were the Marines that died on that bridge with their bayonets fixed. We had pre-plotted artillery and mortar fire all around us, but if the enemy got too close, artillery and mortar fire would do no good. As we began to dig in, I noticed everyone was not acting as scared as I was. Maybe they were just trying to act unafraid, but I didn't pretend at all. I told Frank

I was scared shitless. He told me to just stay down and call in the pre-plots as I was taught if the shit hit the fan. Then he said if we were going to be overrun, for me to call the fire directly on top of us, called danger close. He did not want any of us captured like the Marine on the bridge; we would rather die fighting than become a POW.

Everyone was on high alert. Somewhere around 0300 hours, we started hearing movement. We could hear it was a large unit, and it seemed like they were not making any effort to keep quiet. They were in a hurry. The good thing was they were moving north of our position and would miss us by a hundred meters or so. To my astonishment, they were using flashlights to see with. They were in a hurry.

Frank gave a spot report to the rear area. He was told to start calling in artillery fire if it seemed they would change direction and head towards us. They had pre-plotted artillery along the river. The enemy would have to get across the river and that was when we were to call it in. They wanted to catch them trying to cross. That would be where they would probably bunch up, and we could get some decent kills. About that time, all hell broke loose to our left. Mike R. was firing like a mad man as were the two Marines to his left. Frank got on the radio and immediately called for fire in that location. Then suddenly the entire perimeter opened up. We were firing with all we had. Several hand grenade explosions went off. The artillery fired some pre-plots and the mortars fired illumination so we could see.

That was when I saw Mike R. digging madly with his entrenching tool. It appeared as if he was trying to dig his hole deeper. I would not find out until the next morning that he was engaged in hand to hand combat with a sapper that had gotten into our perimeter. He had killed the sapper with his entrenching tool. As the battle continued, I noticed everyone concentrating fire in a small area of brush to my left front. That's where the larger amount of fire was coming from. Our machine gunner was laying death and destruction down on the enemy trying to get into our perimeter.

Apparently, the enemy that hit us was a small element used for flank security of the main force, or at least that's what we figured. Frank called in the pre-plotted fire along the edge of the river, where we figured the main force was trying to cross. By now, we had ceased firing and all we could do was watch. Every now and then, someone from inside the perimeter would fire a couple of rounds into the bushes, but received no return fire. Frank was busy moving from position to position, making sure everyone was okay and redistributing ammo. We continued the fire missions to keep the enemy off balance. Frank was called and told to move to another location. He told the caller he would, but then explained to me we weren't moving. It was just too risky. They only wanted us to move about a hundred meters south of our current location, but Frank knew there wasn't any good cover there, so we stayed put. He had disobeyed the commander, but had looked after us, again.

It started to get light out, but in the jungle it was hard to tell. A dense fog had set in, and we were still trying to watch out for the enemy. That's when I noticed Mike R. He was throwing something out of his hole. It was the body of the enemy soldier he had killed the night before. The body had no head. He had decapitated the man with his entrenching tool during his fight. He then held the head up and threw it down the hill. The rest of the squad was getting their gear gathered up, getting ready to continue the mission. Frank wanted to move at first light while we still had some darkness to cover us. We got the word to saddle up, and we moved out.

I was calling in a sit rep to the company rear when the commander came on the radio and asked to talk to Frank. I handed him the radio. The company commander said the battalion commander wanted us to go and check out the area that was bombed the night before to see if we could get a body count. Frank wasn't thrilled with the idea of going into that area. If there were any casualties left, and if it was as large a force as we suspected, they would be pissed and ready for a fight.

Frank had three guys move out in front of our position and see if we had any bodies or blood trails there first. About fifteen minutes later, they all had reported back and said they did see blood trails headed towards the river north of our location. They found some discarded equipment also and kept them as war souvenirs. The only body was the one Mike had killed and spent all night in the hole with. It was a miracle none of us had a scratch on us. The only wounds would be the mental wounds we all received and would suffer with the rest of our lives—especially Mike.

Frank decided we would not follow the blood trails but instead move around them about a hundred meters and work our way to the river. Frank took point himself, with me right behind. I was nervous because it was obvious that Frank did not want to go check for bodies just for the sake of a body count for the battalion commander. We moved very deliberately and slowly along the river bank. Frank finally came upon a fresh grave site. It had been hastily dug the night before and most likely contained the bodies of the enemy we had killed that night with artillery. Frank called in a spot report to the company commander and gave him the grid coordinates of the graves. The commander then told Frank to go ahead and continue our mission.

It would take us about four days to move back to Hill 37. When we returned, we had to debrief our platoon commander. He told us the battalion commander wasn't happy that we had not continued after we found the grave site. Of course, it wasn't Frank's decision to not continue but the company commanders. Frank was told that the commander wanted our squad to lead a platoon from another company out to the grave site the next day and that company would continue the search.

We secured for the night, got showers and hot chow, and prepared to get some rest. The other company wanted to move out as soon as possible in the morning. That night Frank became very ill. He was throwing up, had diarrhea, and had a high fever. I helped him over to the medical tent and left him. I got up early the next morning to find the LT to tell him about Frank. I found the LT in the mess tent eating breakfast. He told me he knew about Frank and that Frank had been medevaced to Da Nang earlier that morning. It looked like he had malaria and would not be returning to the unit.

I was devastated. I asked about the patrol we were supposed to take out, and he said the company would just have to find the graves without us. They had the grid coordinates, so it shouldn't be a problem. I went back to our squad tent to tell the guys that Frank had been medevaced. None of them were very happy, especially Mike

R. because that would make him squad leader, and he had less than a month to go and didn't want the responsibility. His mind was fried by then, and he said he just couldn't take it anymore. He said he was going to find the LT and tell him to pick someone else.

About an hour later, the LT came into our tent. He told Marvin he would be the new squad leader if Frank did not return, and Mike would not be going out on any more operations. He had been there over a year by now and, based on what happened two nights earlier, he would be going home. Mike would never be the same after that. He just kind of sat around in a daze. He finally went home while we were out on another patrol about two weeks later.

Our squad was now down to five Marines. We were placed on stand down until replacements could be found. We would do hole watch duties for the next week or two until we could get back up to strength.

Not long after, we were relieved from hole watch, ate breakfast, and returned to our tent. When we walked in, there was Frank. He looked like death warmed over. He said he didn't like the hospital in Da Nang, so he got dressed, walked outside and caught a ride back to the hill. I asked him what had happened, and he said he was just sick as hell. He had not been properly released from the hospital, but that didn't matter to him. He just wanted out. He went to report to the LT and then went to our corpsman to get some medicine to help him out. We were really glad to see him back, especially Marvin.

The next day, we were assigned duty as security for a mine sweeping detail between Hill 37 and Hill 55. This would be the first time I'd been back on Liberty Road since I first got there and was ambushed. I didn't like Liberty Road anymore than anyone else. We had picked up two new replacements and had seven guys in the squad again. It's funny but, I don't remember any of their names. Frank was still weak from being sick, but insisted on going on the road sweep. The LT told him to get in the back of the truck and ride instead of walk, or he would keep him in the rear. That was okay with Frank, so he and I got in the back of the truck.

It was the same type of road sweep we had been on previously, with the engineers and their mine sweeping equipment. This time we had one tank, the engineers, one big truck, and our squad of Marines for security. Frank was on the right side of the truck, and I was on the left. I had my radio on my back and was monitoring the company radio frequency, watching the left side of the road for enemy activity. I remember I was singing "Day Dream Believer" by the Monkeys to myself. We were almost to the dog-leg in the road where I had been ambushed a couple of months before, when *boom*. An explosion blew up the truck. The tire I had been sitting directly over had hit a huge mine. The force of the explosion blew me out of the back of the truck. It blew Frank out the right side of the truck. It knocked me out for a few seconds, I woke up without my weapon in my hand. I still had the radio hand set in my hand, but no weapon. I was lying on my back on top of my radio. All I could see was dirt and dust, and I smelled the truck burning. Someone grabbed me by the harness of my radio back pack and dragged me away from the truck. I could hear firing going off, but I was still in a daze. There was a tremendous ringing in my left ear, and I couldn't hear out of it.

I looked over to my right and saw Frank lying there unconscious. The corpsman was next to him putting a bandage around his head. Frank had a small gash in the side of his head, probably from where part of the truck hit him. I was still woozy when the corpsman came over to me. He kept saying that I would be okay. I kept asking for my weapon. Finally, someone came over and handed it to me. The firing ceased, and everyone formed a perimeter around the blown up truck while the corpsman was wrapping my right arm with a field dressing. Apparently, I had been hit by flying shrapnel that cut my right wrist pretty good. I could see blood coming from the bandage, but it didn't seem to hurt. I couldn't feel a thing, but my head hurt like hell.

I sat up and someone had took my radio off my back. It had a gaping hole in it where a big piece of shrapnel hit it. If I had not been wearing the radio, the shrapnel would have more than likely gotten me in the back. The radio saved me from serious injury, or death. Frank was coming around by now. He tried to stand, but staggered and fell back down. The corpsman told me to stay put and not to try to stand up. He went over and assisted Frank to his feet. Frank came over to me to see if I was okay. A reaction force had been called to come and assist us. I found out later the truck driver had been killed. He got hit in the head by some flying shrapnel. I didn't know him, but I still felt bad for him.

Not long after, the reaction force showed up. Frank and I were put in a field ambulance and taken back to Hill 37. The squad finished the road sweep to Hill 55 with the reaction force. Frank and I were in the medical tent when the company commander came in and told Frank that was his second Purple Heart and then told me it would be my first Purple Heart. My brain was still fuzzy from the explosion, and what he had told me didn't really sink in. We were told we both had concussions and our headaches would last for a couple of days. We didn't know if our hearing would ever come back. To this day, I cannot hear out of my left ear without the use of a hearing aid. My right ear also sustained damage and I have a hearing aid for that ear, too. I was diagnosed with tinnitus in my left ear. The ringing would always be there, and there was nothing I could do about it but get used to it.

That night, both Frank and I had terrible headaches, so Frank told one of the new guys to go find our corpsman. He came into our tent, and Frank told him he had to give us something for our headaches besides aspirin. The corpsman kind of looked around and handed us each two little blue pills. I have no idea what they were. He told us to take them and to lie down, and not get up or move around. We took them, and, within five minutes, I was out. I didn't wake up until about 1000 hours the next morning. If there had been a mortar or rocket attack during the night, I don't think I would have woken up. I was *that* knocked out. I looked over and Frank wasn't on his rack. I still felt like crap, but got up because I was hungry as hell. It was still too early for lunch, so I decided to go to the showers. Frank was in the shower still looking bad. He said he did feel a little better and would be okay. That was good news. He still had to answer to the commander for leaving the hospital without being released, but he didn't care.

It was ironic that the mine detector had already passed over the mine that blew up the truck. I guess you can't really rely on mine detectors after all.

As we continued to regain our strength, we were preparing for our next mission that would forever change my, and many others, lives.

CHAPTER 10

LIBERTY BRIDGE:

GOOD-BYE, FRANK

So, they got us surrounded; now we can fire in any direction. Those bastards won't get away this time!

– Chesty Puller, USMC

We remained around Hill 37 for the next week or so, running patrols and ambushes there. Not much happened during that time. I was receiving mail regularly now and that was good. I knew Frank didn't have much time left in country, so I asked him if he was going to come out of the field any time soon. He told me if he left, we would all turn into shit birds, and he couldn't go out like that. He said he would remain with the squad until the day he left. That was good news to hear.

A few days later, all the squad leaders had a big meeting with the LT. We knew something was up because they never had meetings like this without something big about to happen. Frank came in and called us all together. He said the company was going to move out and go secure Liberty Bridge. Liberty Bridge was the only bridge in that area that crossed the river and it led to An Hoa Marine base. The road went right through the Arizona Territory, the badest land in our area of operation. Nobody liked going into the Arizona with anything less than a platoon or company of Marines. The area was heavily mined and booby trapped and was a major infiltration route for the NVA. For this mission, we would conduct patrols and ambushes on both sides of the river, as well as provide security for the Seabees that were rebuilding the bridge. (Seabees are Navy combat construction engineers that can build anything, anywhere.) The VC seemed to blow up this bridge every chance they got.

By now, Frank decided it was time to train another RTO. He knew I was getting tired of carrying the radio, even though I really didn't mind the job. I got my trusty M14 back and was happy about that. We would alternate carrying the radio, so one guy didn't get too burnt out. I was to train the new guy on proper radio procedures. I think Frank was thinking ahead because we seemed to be doing a lot of cross training on all the equipment: Machine guns, M79 grenade launcher, and communications. He was getting us ready for when he left, making sure everyone knew all he could teach them so anyone of us to take over. I didn't have to worry about taking over anything, with my track record so far.

I didn't like moving away from Hill 37. I liked it there and felt secure, even though the hill was constantly being hit by rocket and mortar fire. I was getting used to having hot chow and warm showers, or any shower at all for that fact. The shower at the water tower was heated by the sun, so if there was no sun, there were no warm showers. It would be a different life at Liberty Bridge.

The day finally came when we moved to the bridge. We road marched there (it really wasn't that far), but we had to go down Liberty Road. Both times I had been on Liberty Road something bad happened. First, the ambush when I arrived. Then the truck blowing up with me in it, so I was very uncomfortable. We moved out early that morning. Thank God our platoon wasn't the lead platoon. We moved at a pretty brisk pace. We were walking down the road when it was decided that we would take a rest. We stopped for about ten minutes. The platoon commanders had a short meeting, and it was decided Third Herd would take the lead the rest of the way to the bridge. I didn't like that at all.

Our squad took the lead. Frank put me on point with one of the new guys. I was on one side of the road and the new guy was on the other side. His name was Moran. Moran was the type of guy you couldn't forget. This guy had me worried. I thought I was a shit bird when I got there, but this guy was worse than I was. He was constantly doing dumb things. I tried to tell him about how bad I screwed up, but he never listened.

As we continued, we were about to come up to the dog-leg in the road where everything bad seemed to happen. Nothing seemed out of the ordinary. As we came up to that point, we saw something in the middle of the road. It was an American helmet. It reminded me of the time I lost my helmet three months earlier. I kind of laughed to myself, thinking how coincidental it would be if it were mine. I saw it and gave the hand signal for the company to halt. We were always taught not to pick stuff up because it could be booby trapped, especially along Liberty Road. I was moving slowly towards the helmet to check it out, when I saw Moran jogging past me to my right. I told him to stay where he was so I could check it out, but he ignored me and continued on. Frank came up about that time to see what was going on.

He saw Moran and yelled for him to stop. Moran ignored Frank too. As Moran got to the helmet, Frank and I hit the dirt. If it was booby trapped, we didn't want to get hit by flying debris. Moran just ignored us; so if it blew up, he would probably get killed. Moran reached down and picked up the helmet. It was not booby trapped. It was his lucky day. He looked back at us and grinned real big and said, "See guys! It's okay." Frank was pissed. Frank grabbed the helmet from Moran and handed it to me. He started yelling at Moran and told him he was sending him to a CAP unit; he just wasn't safe and was going to get someone killed.

I examined the helmet closely, and, of course, it wasn't mine. I had written my girlfriend's name on my helmet's camo cover, and this one didn't have any writing on it. Frank moved Moran to the end of the squad, and we continued on to Liberty Bridge. Frank stayed on point with me the rest of the way.

The rest of the movement went well. We got to the bridge and replaced the company occupying it. They headed back to Hill 37 the same way we had come, straight down Liberty Road. About an hour after they left, we heard gun fire. They had been ambushed going back to Hill 37. We were put on immediate alert in case they needed help. They had casualties, but we didn't know how many. The firefight lasted about fifteen minutes, then it was all over. I was just glad it wasn't us. They didn't need our help, so we continued to start our new mission on the bridge.

Frank went to meet up with the LT to tell him of his concerns with Moran. The LT talked to the company commander and made the decision to send Moran back to Hill 37 to be assigned to a CAP unit. The battalion commander had been pressured by brigade to fill the CAP's, so it was perfect timing. Each platoon had to send one man each, and Moran was ours. We had lost a new man, but, in this case, we were happy. I don't know if Moran ever made it through his tour or not. I know the CAP units were overrun a couple more times when I was there, but I never heard the names of the casualties. More than likely, Moran did not make it. There are several Morans on the Vietnam Memorial Wall. One of those names is probably his.

Since the bridge was still being built by the Seabees, we had to guard both sides of the bridge. The west side of the bridge would be guarded by just one platoon. It was only accessible by barge since the bridge wasn't finished. The rest of the company would remain on the east side of the bridge with the Seabees. They would conduct most of the patrols and night ambushes.

The west side platoon would conduct daily squad patrols into the Arizona, not going too far out because of the danger. Those patrols were used mainly to look for fresh enemy activity. It was not unusual for the west side platoon to get harassment fire and probes during the night, so it was pretty intense on the west side, and there was only one platoon over there to boot. The good thing about being on the east side was the Seabees had a sweet setup over there. They used their big bulldozers to dig in the tents and the fighting positions. It was great having added extra heavy equipment. If we needed a new hole dug, we just called the Seabee platoon sergeant, and it was dug. We also used their big equipment to push back the jungle, creating a larger open area in front of our positions so it would be harder for the enemy to sneak up on us. The best thing they had, though, was great chow. This was the first time during my tour (and the last) that I could actually get red Kool-Aid. I was excited. They also had excellent shower facilities. It was then I thought, *Maybe I should have joined the Navy like my mom wanted me to do.*

Our platoon stayed on the east side for the first part of the mission. First Platoon drew the duty for the west side of the bridge, which made me very happy. I was in no hurry to be on the west side of the bridge. We were notified by the LT that our squad was going to conduct the first three day recon mission, starting out the next morning. We were short a man again because we had sent Moran back to Hill 37, so I was picked to carry the radio. No problem. I had done it for awhile now and become pretty accustomed to it. Frank decided we would have a squad meeting that night to go over what we would be doing during the next few days. He would also check all our equipment as we were going to leave at first light the next morning.

Just before going to chow that evening, I was talking with Marvin and asked him if he thought I was ever going to be promoted to lance corporal (E-3). He jokingly said that, based on my history when I first got there, that he didn't know if I'd ever get promoted, but he would talk to Frank about it. He went to the other end of the tent and was talking to Frank when they both started laughing. I figured I was destined to stay a private first class (E-2) my entire time in Kilo Company.

That evening at chow, everyone was tense. Patrols were going to start going out the next morning and everyone seemed on edge. I was laughing and joking with a friend of mine who was sitting at the other end of the tent, when he started flipping me off, giving me the finger, so I returned the gesture several times. This went on a little while when this huge Navy guy came over and asked me why I was giving him the finger. This guy looked like a mountain. I tried to explain that I was flipping off my buddy, but he wouldn't hear of it. He told me he would meet me outside when I finished eating. Of course, I thought maybe someone had put him up to this to scare me, but that was not the case.

As I got up to take my tray outside, there was the big Navy guy standing there with his buddy. Ricky and I put down our trays and tried to walk away, but he stood in my way.

I said, "Look, I wasn't flipping you off," and tried again to move around him.

He pushed me, and I knew I was about to get an ass-whooping. I weighed all of 125 pounds soaking wet and this guy looked to weigh 200 pounds and not a bit of it fat. Well, being the big bad Marine, I thought, *Here we go*. I was not about to back down. About that time, he hauled off and knocked the shit out of me. I fell to the ground, and the fight was over. All I could see were stars. Ricky helped me up and the Navy guy told me I had better watch who I was flipping off next time. I guess he forgot all about the fact we carried weapons there. Or maybe it didn't matter to him.

As we walked back to the tent—well, Ricky walked, I staggered—Ricky was laughing at me and told me that was the fastest fight he had ever seen. We got back to the tent and saw Frank and Marvin and a couple of other guys standing outside smoking. They looked at my left eye and started laughing. They asked what the hell hit me.

Laughing, Ricky said, "Tack let a Navy guy whip his ass at the chow tent."

They asked if I got any punches in, but all Ricky could say through his laughter was that, "All the Navy guy got out of it was a skinned knuckle, and it was Tack's skin."

Frank sent me to the corpsman to make sure I was okay and told me to stay the hell away from the Seabees from now on. He also made a comment about how I wanted a promotion, but I couldn't even whip a squid (what we called Navy guys). I never could explain to any of them that I didn't do anything to him. I also tried telling them the guy was huge, but they wouldn't listen. I had been whipped by a squid. I did see the Navy guy in the chow tent about a week later, and he ask if I was okay and said he was sorry. We had a good laugh over it, and I had a black eye and a great story to tell my fellow Marines. Of course, my version was I had held my own against the monster squid.

The next morning I woke up with a huge headache and my eye almost swollen shut.

Frank asked me if I wanted to stay behind from the patrol, but I said, "No, I will be okay. We are already short-handed."

There was no way I was going to miss out going on the first recon mission because of a fight. We got our final briefing from the LT, and we were off. We were to recon about 500 meters north, stop, set up a night ambush on a well used trail, and then loop back the next day, reconning around the bridge for another day. It was easy moving through the area north of the bridge. The jungle didn't seem as dense. It was a near perfect day. Not too hot, just right. I was starting to get a little lax. It just seemed like a walk in the park. We stopped several times, and I called in the pre-plotted check points as we rested. There didn't seem to be any new signs of enemy activity anywhere. Sometime around 1800 hours that evening, Frank decided we would stop one more time, eat, then move into our ambush site just after dark. Frank and Ricky moved forward to scout out the ambush site. Frank told me to call in a sit rep of what was going on while he was gone.

I called the LT on our platoon radio frequency just after Frank and Ricky departed and gave him the sit rep basically just saying we were laying low until time to move into position, which was normal procedure. The LT then asked for our location. Without thinking, I committed the ultimate sin for a radio operator. I sent him our location in the clear. In other words, I didn't encode the map coordinates. I just sent the LT our exact location, so anyone listening could hear and understand. There was a couple of minutes of silence, then the LT came back on the radio. He said that I had just told the enemy where we were, and I had compromised the patrol. He told me to have Frank call him as soon as he got back from his recon.

Marvin came over and asked me what the hell did I just do. I told him, and he wasn't happy. He told everyone to pack up; we were going to move as soon as Frank got back.

I was devastated. I had gotten lazy and stupid. I could have gotten our entire squad killed. *What the hell was I thinking*? I knew we had to encode grid coordinates, but I just didn't do it. Frank and Ricky returned about thirty minutes later. Marvin explained what happened, and I told him the LT wanted him to call him immediately. Frank was pissed (as he should have been). The LT told us to abort our mission and to move to another location to spend the night. He told us to find a good hiding place since I had told anyone listening where we were. If the enemy was listening, they would be looking for us. He then told Frank to take the radio from me and give it to someone else.

I felt like shit. All the trust and confidence I had built up with my squad had been destroyed in a moment of laziness. Nobody talked the rest of the night. We moved east about 200 meters, Frank found a big stand of bamboo to hide in. We moved carefully into it, set up our claymore mines and remained there the rest of the night. We moved out of the bamboo thicket at first light the next morning, being careful to hide the fact we were even there. It took us most of the day to get back to Liberty Bridge since we moved in a series of dog-legs, instead of heading there in a straight line. Of course, I was walking point. When we got back, Frank told us to secure our gear and get some chow. He would go brief the LT. I knew I would probably have to go see the company commander—my status as a shit bird re-confirmed. I also knew the battalion was still sending Marines to the CAP units and that worried the hell out of me. *Will I be next?*

The next day, our squad was put on hole watch. We would be on hole watch for a few days, then the entire platoon would move to the west side of the bridge. Frank assigned me to a bunker with one of the new guys. I think his name was Lee. He was a tough acting black kid from Chicago. He had only been there about a week, and the patrol the day before was his first. He had no idea what was going on and asked what had happened. I told him I had fucked up really bad. I also told him that my time in Third Herd was probably limited because of how bad I had screwed up since I got there. I told him he had better not follow my example or he would be right there with me.

About that time, Frank came up to the bunker. I hadn't talked to him since the patrol, and I knew he wasn't happy with me. We went to the back of the bunker, and he told me the LT and platoon sergeant had enough of me. I had really screwed up this time. They wanted to send me to Office Hours in front of the company commander and send me to the rear for re-assignment. Frank said he argued with them about it because he saw some redeeming qualities in me. He told them he would watch me like a hawk, and besides, he was short-handed as it was and couldn't afford to lose one more man. We only had seven Marines in our squad. The LT finally gave in and let me stay with the squad, but he did say that was my last shot. If I ever screwed up again, I was gone.

Of course, the platoon sergeant had the last word. You guessed it: I went on shit burning detail again. I didn't argue, I knew I had screwed up bad, and it was the least I expected would happen to me. I figured I would be sent to a CAP with Moran for sure. I also knew I had sealed my fate for my promotion, too. I would remain a PFC forever.

The next few days went by without incident. I burned the shitters every day without complaint and pulled hole watch during the night. I mainly stayed to myself, feeling really bad. The day before we moved across the river to the west side, we had a big platoon meeting. The LT briefed us on our mission over there and said there was a lot of enemy activity and we had better be on our toes. Several patrols from the other company had casualties from booby traps, and they had been probed several nights by sappers trying to find weaknesses in the defense.

After the LT's meeting, the squad got together for a final equipment check. Frank got up in front of the squad and said we had to forget about the incident on the patrol and that I would again be his squad radio operator. Despite what I had done, I was still the best radio operator in the squad and he wanted me. That was a great boost to my confidence, and I told him I wouldn't let him down. He said he knew I wouldn't because if I did, he would slit my throat, pulling his thumb across his throat as if to make a cutting motion, then he grinned at me. All had been forgiven. I asked if I could say something. I apologized to the squad and told them I would never get lazy again. They were all okay with me. I was almost in tears when I apologized. I was still only an eighteen-year-old kid.

The next day the platoon moved across the river and performed what they called a relief in place. That meant as one squad moved into position, the other squad would get them settled in, show them their direction of fire, get them familiar with the terrain, and then the other squad would depart. The weather started turning crappy, raining a lot. Monsoon season wasn't supposed to come in until around May, but it made an early appearance, we were wet all the time. We settled in to our new digs. Our area of responsibility was looking to the northwest. If I remember right, using a clock as a reference, we had from about the twelve o'clock to the three o'clock position.

The platoon headquarters was in a big bunker, roughly in the middle of the perimeter. It certainly wasn't as comfortable as the east side of the river. We didn't have showers over there as I recall either—we had to use our helmets to wash. By now, I was used to not showering for a long time, so that didn't really bother me. I had already assumed I would be on shit burning detail every day, but Frank told me since I was the radio operator again, I would not have to burn shit anymore. I was relieved. The new guy Lee was pissed, though, because now he had to do it.

As we got into our daily routine, I made sure I did not turn lazy. I cleaned my radios daily, checked and insured I had all my extra equipment for them and extra batteries. I studied the CEOI with a vengeance. I could encode and decode messages, encode grid coordinates, and use proper radio procedure with the best of them. Frank even had me giving radio procedure classes to the new guys. I felt normal again. I knew my chances of ever being promoted were slim to none and accepted that. I had done all of this to myself and had nobody to blame but me. I knew I wasn't going to be a career Marine, so it really didn't make a big difference anyway. I just wanted to do my best to not disappoint Frank and the squad ever again.

We were told we would be on the west side of the bridge for about a week to ten days. I saw a new staff NCO at the headquarters bunker when I went there for the RTO meetings. He was a black Marine I had never seen. I was told his name was Staff Sergeant Thompson (or Thomas, I really don't remember). I didn't see the old platoon sergeant and guessed that he had, most likely, gone home and this guy was his replacement. I figured he had probably briefed the new staff sergeant about me, so I steered clear of the guy. It surprised me that the new staff sergeant never seemed to want to come out of the command bunker. He would only come out for very short periods of time to check the perimeter, then return to the command bunker. Our old platoon sergeant was always out on the perimeter and that was reassuring to me—even though the guy didn't like me. This new guy wasn't like that.

There were three daily patrols that we had to run. One of the patrols was checking the road that led from the perimeter down to the river, where a small Navy barge would land to carry supplies over to us. It wouldn't take very long to do the patrol down to the barge. It was not even a hundred meters, but the VC had a habit of booby trapping the road at night, we had to clear it so we could receive our supplies.

On the second or third day there, one of the other squads was patrolling west of the perimeter when I heard a loud explosion. I was at our bunker monitoring the radio. The squad hit a booby trap, and had a casualty. A small fire fight ensued, but ended within five or ten minutes. I listened on the radio as the squad in contact talked to the LT. The wounded Marine could walk out and there was no need for a medevac helicopter to come and get him. The perimeter was put on high alert until they returned.

About an hour later, they walked back into the perimeter. The wounded Marine was okay. He had received a small shrapnel wound behind his knee. He was dazed, but none the worse for wear. The LT wanted to have a briefing with all the squad leaders about what the patrol had found. During the briefing, the squad leader of the patrol explained that they couldn't walk very far without encountering booby traps. They were everywhere. They would clear them as they moved, but then would come upon another one. It was very dangerous out there, to say the least. The guy that had gotten wounded had just cleared one booby trap when he tripped another one. He was very lucky he only got a small piece of shrapnel in his leg.

Frank returned to our bunker to brief the squad on what he had just heard. We started retraining immediately on how to spot booby traps and how to clear or disarm them. I was glad I was a RTO then, because it was mainly the point man that would have to spot and clear the booby traps. Frank said he didn't have a good feeling at all about this place, and for the first time since I got there, he seemed kind of nervous. I knew he was getting short, but he still wouldn't come out of the field.

A couple of days later, the weather seemed to clear up. We had the patrol responsibility for the road sweep to the barge that morning. I decided to carry my M14. Mike S. took the radio to give me a break. We got to the barge without incident. The small cargo vehicle (called a mule) came off the barge, and we started back to the perimeter with our daily supply of food and water. About half way back, we were ambushed by a small enemy element. The guy driving the mule hauled ass up to the hill as we returned fire. I must have fired four or five magazines of M14 rounds on full automatic before the enemy broke contact with us.

Frank decided to move into the bush to see if we hit anything. He grabbed me and Ricky, and we moved out. About twenty meters into the brush, we found the site where enemy was hiding. There were about a hundred empty AK47 casings lying on the ground and an enemy canteen that a VC soldier had dropped. Frank made sure it wasn't booby trapped and picked it up. He gave it to me, saying it was mine because of all the rounds I had put down. I thanked him; it was my second war trophy. We got back to the hill, and we went straight to our bunker.

The LT and the staff sergeant came over to debrief us. The staff sergeant looked scared to death. Hell, he wasn't even down there with us. Frank told the LT that we were ambushed by a small element of about three to four individuals based on what we found in the bush. He also said there was one blood trail leading off into the jungle and that we had hit something. He had decided not to follow it because there were only three of us. He told the LT I was responsible for making the enemy break contact because I had stood up firing magazine after magazine from my M14. The LT looked at me and said, "Good job, Tack." I didn't know what to say.

That was the first time he had ever said anything kind to me. I was proud as hell. Frank had given me all the credit. I know it was a squad effort, not just me, but Frank was trying to make a point in front of the new staff sergeant. He also told the LT that he was very worried about this place. He did not have a good feeling at all. He knew something was probably going to happen because it was unusual that we would be ambushed on that road that early in the day. The LT concurred and said he didn't much like that area either and we needed to be especially watchful and keep our shit wired until we got back across the river.

Sometime after evening chow, Frank gathered the squad. There were seven of us again. He put Ricky and me together, Marvin and Lee together, and Mike S. and Gary

C. together. We would be on 100 percent alert until further notice. Again, I could tell Frank was nervous. He told Mike S. and Gary to place additional pop flares in the barbed wire in front of our position. Ricky and Marvin were making several booby traps out of hand grenades that they would also place in the wire later on. Just after dark, Marvin and Ricky went to the wire and placed the hand grenade booby traps and two additional claymore mines in the wire. We could retrieve them in the morning if we didn't use them. There was no moon that night, and it was as dark as I'd ever seen it. It was 27 March 1968, and our lives were about to be changed forever.

It was standard operating procedure to go to the platoon CP to get radio instructions for the night at around 2300 hours. We changed frequencies at midnight. It was just a precaution to insure all the squad RTO's were on the right frequency. The new staff sergeant had been making noise, saying he wanted the squad RTO's to pull radio watch in the command bunker so he wouldn't have to. Frank had argued with him that we were already short men on the perimeter and he couldn't afford to leave me down there watching his radios.

Normally, Frank would go down, but tonight he sent me. He wanted to stay with the squad because he had an uneasy feeling. He had been hearing strange noises all night long outside the wire and wanted to stay there. I had been lying down right beside Ricky when Frank told me to go. I grabbed my weapon and started towards the command bunker. As I said, it was dark as hell, and I walked slowly so I wouldn't trip over anything.

I got to the bunker and met up with the other RTO's. The platoon leader's RTO gave us the new frequencies and last minute instructions. I could see the staff sergeant giving us the eye. I suggested we finish up outside, before the sergeant decided to make us stay there and pull his watch. The LT had to go to the east side of the bridge for a meeting with the company commander and would spend the night there. This was the first night the staff sergeant would be by himself. We went out and talked for a few minutes, allowing our eyes to readjust to the darkness. I told the other RTO's to have a good night and started back towards my bunker.

I got about half way back, about twenty meters away, when a loud explosion came from the bunker. Something had blown it up. The entire side of our perimeter opened up. I ran as fast as I could to the bunker, trying to see if anyone was wounded. About the same time, a couple of other guys from the other squads got there, along with the platoon corpsman. Bullets were flying everywhere. I lay down beside Mike S. who was cussing and not firing his weapon. By now, flares were going off in the wire and our booby traps were being set off. We had gooks in the wire. I could see tracers coming in from outside the wire and concentrated my fire there. I looked over and noticed Mike's hand was bleeding. I helped him wrap it with his bandage while continuing to fire. He said a bullet had hit his weapon right at the pistol grip and ruined the trigger housing and it wouldn't fire.

It was then that I saw Frank lying behind the bunker. He was hurt bad. I could also see the corpsman working frantically on someone; I didn't know who. Another guy from another squad was working on Lee who had also been wounded. I gave Mike my weapon and ran to help Frank. He was bleeding everywhere. I grabbed him by his harness and dragged him away from the smoking bunker, behind the berm of dirt the Seabees had built some time before we got there. Bullets continued to fly, but I knew I had to help Frank.

By now, we were receiving artillery flares from Hill 37. The flares really lit up the night; I could really see now how bad it actually was. I saw the corpsman continuing to work on someone; I realized it was Marvin. I couldn't see Ricky or Gary, and didn't know what happened to them. I looked at Frank, he had what looked like a bullet wound to his right arm and a bullet wound to his right leg. The rest of his body was covered with multiple shrapnel wounds. He was bleeding everywhere. I started hollering for the corpsman, but the two that were there were busy.

I took off Frank's 782 gear and tore his blood soaked t-shirt off. I took his field dressing and put it on the wound on his arm the way we were taught in first aid training. Then I took my field dressing and put it on his leg wound. He was drifting in and out of consciousness, and I could tell he was going into shock from the loss of blood. I didn't have any more field dressings, and his chest was bleeding badly. I could see bubbles coming from one of the holes that meant he had a sucking chest wound. One of his lungs had been punctured. I took the discarded plastic from the field dressing and placed it over the hole to seal the wound. I took off my flak jacket and gear, pulled off my t-shirt and held it over Frank's chest in an attempt to stop him from bleeding to death. About that time, the corpsman came running up to me and told me to go to the bunker and help the other guys there, and he would take care of Frank. I didn't want to leave Frank's side, but knew the other guys needed help.

By now, there was only sporadic firing going on around the perimeter. We had fought off the attack. Flares were still going off, so I could still see. The bunker was destroyed. I figured it had been a rifle propelled grenade (RPG) that hit it because of all the damage. Someone was yelling at me to help get Ricky out of the bunker. I jumped in and saw Ricky was dead. He had been killed instantly by the explosion. Not fifteen minutes before that, I had been lying right next to him. If I had been there, I would have been killed, also. We wrapped him in a poncho and moved him to the rear of the bunker. They had Lee propped up against what was left of the bunker. He seemed to be unconscious. I looked over and saw another body covered up with a poncho. It was then that Gary came up to me and told me it was Marvin. The corpsman made a valiant effort to save Marvin, but there was just too much damage.

That must have killed the LT, not being there with his men. The staff sergeant didn't even come out of the command bunker. I didn't see him until the next morning when the LT came back across the river.

Another squad leader was there helping and told me a medevac helicopter was coming in to take out Lee and Frank, and if there was no ground fire, we would load the killed in action also. He told me to grab a flashlight and guide in the helicopter. By that time, the flares stopped going off so it wouldn't light up the incoming medevac. It seemed like it was taking forever for him to get there. I could see the corpsman holding a flashlight, frantically still working on Frank.

About that time, I heard the helicopter coming in. I turned on the flashlight and waved it in the air. He came down slowly almost landing right on top of me. It was then I realized I didn't have anything on above the waist. I had used my t-shirt on Frank. Dirt and debris were flying everywhere, tearing into my chest. I covered my face but held my position and the flashlight up to guide in the chopper. I didn't think we were receiving any ground fire, so I ran over and picked up one end of the poncho that Ricky was in. I reached down to grab it but the wind had blown it open. I grabbed what seemed like mush. It was Ricky's torn-up body. We recovered Ricky and carried him to the helicopter. Two other guys carried Marvin over. I then ran and picked up one end of the litter Frank was on.

The corpsman had been able to get an IV in Frank's arm by then and had his wounds covered. Frank didn't look good. The corpsman said he didn't know if Frank was going to make it. They had already loaded Lee. All of this seemed to take forever, but in reality it probably only lasted about five minutes or less. Mike was not medevaced. He only had a few cuts from where his weapon was blown out of his hand. The helicopter took off, and it was then that I heard firing continuing to go on. That pilot landed knowing it was a hot LZ, but came anyway—there were wounded Marines down there. What guts those guys had. I wish I knew their names. They had probably saved Frank's life, if he was to live.

After the helicopter left, the firing ceased. The other squad leader got a couple of his guys and had them help us on the perimeter until it got light. About an hour later, it hit me. Our entire squad was gone with the exception of Gary, Mike, and myself. What the hell were we going to do now?

The next morning we got a look at the devastation. The LT came up to the bunker to see how we were doing. I was in shock, as were Mike and Gary. He said the platoon was going back to the other side of the river as soon as the other platoon was ready to replace us. He told us to gather up all the equipment and stack it so it could be taken over and separated on the other side. He asked me where my shirt was. I had put my flak jacket back on. I noticed my chest was bleeding, but not bad. He asked if I was wounded, and if I was, it would be my second Purple Heart; one more and I could go home. I told him I thought it was from the dirt and debris thrown up by the medevac. He told me to get it checked out when we got to the other side.

As we began the cleanup, I saw my pack and radio by the bunker. Both had been destroyed by the explosion. I believe to this day that if Frank not sent me to the command bunker that night I would have been killed. Frank had saved my life once again. I had also had two radios destroyed by enemy fire. When I got to the other side, I hoped they wouldn't make me an RTO again.

POST SCRIPT:

I never heard anything from that point on about whether Frank and Lee had survived or not. I was too afraid to go to the Vietnam Memorial website to see if their names were on it. I tried to hide it in the back of my mind for many years.

In July 2006, I got a phone call from Rich Trucker. He told me someone was trying to get a hold of me and to expect a call. I tried to get him to tell me who, and then he said, "Frank."

I said, "Frank who?" and he said, "Frank Powers." I immediately went into shock. Frank had survived. I was so happy I didn't know how to act. I waited by the phone, and about ten minutes later it rang. It was Frank. It was then he told me why he hadn't been looking for me before now.

He said after he was wounded he couldn't remember what had happened. He was in the hospital in Da Nang waiting to get stable enough to be transferred to Japan and out of country. He was hurt really bad. The doctors said he would live, but would have problems the rest of his life. One day, he said, the new staff sergeant came in to visit him and Lee. He didn't know where Lee was, but he wasn't there. He then told me something astonishing. He told me the staff sergeant told him the hill had gotten overrun, and his entire squad was dead. He thought we had all been killed. I could not figure out why the staff sergeant would tell him something like that.

Frank lived with the guilt for thirty-eight years that everyone in his squad but Lee was dead. He said he never forgot us, and the survivor guilt had consumed him since then. I asked him how he found me. He said he was looking through the Disabled American Veteran Magazine and saw a notice for a Kilo Third of the Seventh reunion in New Orleans in August 2006. He wondered if it was the Kilo Third of the Seventh he was assigned to and called the point of contact. He talked to Harry Smith about the upcoming reunion, and yes, it was Frank's Kilo Third of the Seventh. He started asking Harry about who all came to the reunions that he might know. Frank told him when he was in Vietnam and Harry said he might know Rich Trucker.

Frank said, "Yes, Rich was in my squad."

He gave Frank Rich's number. Frank talked to Rich for a long time before he asked him who else came to the reunion that he might know.

It was then that Rich told him, "Well you probably remember Don Tackett."

Frank said he was told I was killed in action (KIA) on the day he was wounded.

Rich said, "No, he comes to the reunions." Frank said he couldn't believe it.

All these years he thought I was dead. He asked Rich about the others, but he didn't know because I was the only one that comes to the reunions.

Frank, his wife, son, and granddaughter came to the New Orleans reunion in August 2006. When Frank and I saw each other, we both cried like a couple of babies. We talked and talked. I could see all the activity was taking a toll on Frank; he was in pain and had to go to bed. I met his wife and son later while Frank was resting. They wanted to know what had happened the night Frank was wounded because Frank could not remember. They only knew it affected him his entire life. We had a long conversation, and I explained to them exactly what happened on 27 March 1968. They didn't have a clue.

Later the next day, we were in the hospitality suite talking. Frank had a sack with him. He pulled out his green squad note book all the squad leaders carried. He showed me how they had to keep information on each of his squad members. If they were wounded or killed, he would put an X over their name and the date. He had put an X over everyone's name that was in the squad on that date and wrote, 27 March 1968 next to the names. He also pulled out an OD green t-shirt and gave it to me. He said somehow he remembered me pulling off my t-shirt during the fire fight and covering his chest with it, and this shirt was to replace it. I couldn't believe he remembered that. Frank said I saved his life that night. I considered it payback for all the times he saved mine.

Frank and I now talk regularly. He lived in Florida, only twenty miles from where my mother lived before she passed away in 2004. Had I known that, I would have visited him every time I went down that way. Frank passed away at his home in Florida on 14 January 2013. He was, and still is, my hero.

CHAPTER 11

DISEASE OF UNKNOWN ORIGIN

Retreat? Hell, we just got here.

– CPT Lloyd Williams, USMC

The platoon replacing us showed up around lunch time. They didn't look too happy. We were supposed to be over there for another week. What was left of our squad was considered combat ineffective. We had lost all our leaders, our squad leader, and both team leaders, along with one rifleman. The three of us that were left had no experience leading a squad. We had all our gear packed up and the LT sent the mule to come to the blown up bunker to get the extra equipment. I was able to piece together enough equipment to last me until we got back to Hill 37. The mule had a whole bunch of new sand bags that had to be filled so the blown up bunker could be rebuilt. I was glad I wasn't on that detail, but felt sure I probably had done something wrong the night before and would be on shit burning detail on the other side of the river.

We made our movement to the other side without any problems. We got settled into the platoon tent when the LT and platoon sergeant ordered Mike, Gary, and me to his tent. He told us what we were expecting to hear. He was moving us to other squads until enough Marines could be found to rebuild our squad. We all asked if we could go back to third squad when it was ready, but he said probably not. We were going to be filling in for Marines that were leaving, and they needed to have continuity in the squads and not move everyone around all the time.

I was assigned to the squad leader that helped in the bunker that night. Mike and Gary went to another squad. I was very familiar with three members of my new squad. One was none other than the joker, Mike R. from Indiana. He smiled really big when I came in. The other two guys were Bobby C. from Texas, and Steve D. from Missouri. I was close to both those guys, especially Steve. We had hung around together when we were back at Hill 37. We had more in common with each other than anyone else. We were about the same age, we had the same interests, and we talked all the time about our girlfriends. We also came from similar backgrounds. Everyone called Steve "Cherry boy," not because he had just gotten to Vietnam; he had been there longer than me. They called him that because he was a virgin, or at least he said he was. He was extremely shy and would blush when guys would tease him about sex. They would try to show him dirty magazines, but he would have nothing to do with it. It was all in good fun. Everyone respected his beliefs, and besides that, he was a hell of a good Marine. He had a baby face that made him look like he was only thirteen years old when he was actually eighteen.

Steve always carried a blue camping style cooking pan. When we had the chance, we would combine our C-ration meals together in his pan and make up our own dinner menus. Surprisingly enough, they were quite good. With the right amount of hot sauce, anything can taste good. Steve and I became inseparable. We were always together. I think he brought out the best in me. He was always squared away. All the time I was with him, I was never put on shit burning detail. I followed his example and it worked.

A guy they called "Rock" was my team leader. I never knew his real name. He was an outstanding team leader. He was a no nonsense kind of guy. All business in the field. One day, about a week later, I had just gotten off hole watch. Rock called me over and said the LT and the platoon sergeant wanted to see me. He asked me what I had done wrong. I told him I didn't remember doing anything wrong. I thought I was doing pretty well. One good thing about my new squad was that nobody in the squad, including the squad leader, held anything against me. It was a fresh start. Everyone knew of my screw-ups in third squad, but everyone was okay with me as long as I did my job.

I could not imagine why the LT wanted to see me. As we entered his tent, I reported as I was taught (especially when I was in trouble). They all started laughing at me because I thought I was in trouble. The LT began to explain to me that Frank and Marvin had been trying to get me promoted to lance corporal (E-3) before he was wounded and Marvin was killed. He said Frank and Marvin were always bothering him about it, so he finally said okay. I was promoted to lance corporal with an effective date of 1 April 1968. Even though I was a huge screw up in third squad, Frank and Marvin still took care of me and got me promoted. What guys. What team leaders. That's how you take care of your troops, a lesson I would carry over into my career. My number one responsibility is to take care of my troops.

It wasn't long after that we were informed we would be moving back to Hill 37. I was relieved; I was ready to get the hell off this bridge. I had been in Vietnam four months by now, and I had already seen too much. I find it necessary to keep reminding my readers that I was still only eighteen years old. In my first four months in country, I had seen too much death and destruction already. I didn't know how I was going to make another nine months and keep my sanity.

We continued to run small patrols off the east side of the river. Two nights before we were to head back to Hill 37, I pulled hole watch with Steve. We were on 50 percent alert, so one of us was awake and one was asleep. It was hot, so whoever slept, slept behind the bunker on the ground, not in the bunker. I didn't want to have anything to do with being inside a bunker because of what happened across the river. Steve woke me around midnight for my two hour watch. We talked for a few minutes on top of the bunker about nothing in particular. He just wanted to make sure I was completely awake. Steve would have stayed up and talked with me my entire watch if he had any idea I was tired and might fall asleep on watch—a major sin. I would have done the same for him.

After about ten minutes, Steve got off the top of the bunker and lay down behind it to catch some Z's. I was on watch for maybe an hour when I started feeling really bad. I got the cold sweats, I was nauseous, and I started getting dizzy. Suddenly, without any warning, I passed out. I must have fallen backwards on top of Steve behind the bunker because I remember hearing Steve hollering at me to get the hell off of him before I passed out again. That was the first and last time I ever heard him cuss. The next thing I remember, I woke up in the medical tent with an IV hanging out of each arm. The corpsman on duty came up to me and asked how I was feeling. I don't remember saying anything, but I knew I had to pee really bad. The senior corpsman came over and handed the other corpsman a bed pan and told me to try to pee in it. I must have made a mess because they had to get me up and move me to another rack. I promptly passed out again. I don't know how long I was out, but when I woke up again, I noticed light coming in from the door of the tent. A different corpsman came up to me and asked again if I was okay. I was still dizzy, but feeling better. I had no idea what was going on and got a little scared. About that time the senior corpsman came up and told me that I had them all worried.

Apparently, when they carried me into the medical tent the night before, my blood pressure was really low, my breathing was shallow, I was cold and clammy, and they had no idea what was going on. At first, they thought I might have been bitten by a snake, or some kind of insect, but after stripping me and examining my entire body, that was ruled out. All they knew was that I was one sick Marine. They couldn't medevac me until I was stable. They thought I was stable enough by then, but couldn't medevac me by helicopter. Instead, I was going to be sent back to Hill 37 when the road sweep team got there and they would put me in a field ambulance back to Hill 37. All I was thinking was, *Oh boy, Liberty Road again!*

Finally, the road sweep team arrived. I was put in the field ambulance with the two IV's still attached to my arms.

I asked for my weapon, but was told, "No, you won't need it." I felt naked without it. Your weapon becomes part of you, you are never without it—especially going down Liberty Road.

The ambulance driver, along with two other vehicles, started down Liberty Road, and they didn't slow down until we got to Hill 37. That was the fastest ride down that road I had ever taken. I remember arriving at the battalion aid station where they were waiting for me. I was taken into the intake room for triage. The battalion surgeon came in looking at the folder the corpsman had sent along with me. He did a complete examination that included another look at my entire body to see if I had been bitten by anything. He asked me questions such as: Had I been to the village lately? Had I been with any of the business girls? Had I drank any of their liquor or beer? Of course, I hadn't. I hadn't been down to the village at all since I'd been in country, except on the medical missions that we would escort down there. I found the questions funny, but he didn't. He said there were all kind of diseases out there that could cause my symptoms. I asked what he thought was wrong with me, but he didn't have a clue. He said it could be anything from malaria to some yet unknown disease, and that I would be medevaced by the first available helicopter to the NSA hospital in Da Nang for further evaluation.

I stayed in the battalion aid station one more sleepless night. The aid station was heavily fortified, because if the hill was mortared or rocketed, it would take time to move the injured into the safe bunkers built around it. That night two mortar rounds hit the hill. They both hit on the opposite side of the hill from the aid station, so we remained in our racks. I was there with three other Marines. Two had been slightly wounded and were waiting to be released back to their units. The other was sick like me, only not as bad. The next morning, I was loaded on a litter jeep and taken to the landing zone to await the helicopter. I wondered to myself if this was my ticket out of Vietnam. I was certainly hoping so. If I made it out of this place in one piece, I would be one happy Marine.

The helicopter finally arrived and we took off, heading for Da Nang. I was still feeling bad, but if this was going to get me the hell out of there, then so be it. It was a short flight into Da Nang. The chopper landed, and I was carried into a triage room. This time, a team of two doctors and two nurses attended to me. These were the first round-eyed women I had seen in over four months.

The doctors seemed concerned about my condition, but all I could focus on were the two nice looking nurses prodding and poking me while they removed my nasty clothes and put me in a hospital gown. I thought for a minute I would get a pudgy (physically excited), but at that point I just didn't care. I was too sick to worry about a little thing like a pudgy, and I'm sure they saw plenty of them in their business. The doctors changed out my IVs to some sort of medication and moved me into a ward of wounded soldiers and Marines. I felt really guilty while lying there. There were guys in there who had really been hurt bad. Some with head wounds, some without limbs, and a couple like me who didn't have any visible injuries at all, just IV's sticking out of their arms.

The guy in the bed next to me was an Army guy. He had been shot in the chest, but the bullet went right through without hurting any major organs. He said he had a million dollar wound. He would fully recover and was being sent home. He was a nice guy; he was a grunt like me and was wounded on a night ambush. We talked for a long time before I must have passed out. When I woke up, it was dark. The nurse was standing over me taking my vital signs. She said they were worried because my blood pressure dropped dramatically again and that's why I passed out. I was going to be moved to another ward, one with guys with infectious diseases. I said good-bye to my new Army friend and was wheeled off.

After a few days of recovering in my new ward, I was feeling much better. One of the IV's was removed, but the other was left in. I was still weak as hell and could stand, but I couldn't walk without assistance. The doctors still didn't know what was wrong with me. One evening, the doctor came in and told me I was being sent out to a hospital ship that was off the coast of Da Nang, and from there would probably be sent to Okinawa or Japan for recovery. He said my time in Nam was over. I was happy as hell. I was going home. I wanted to call or write home as soon as possible, but was told I should probably wait a couple of days and see what happened.

About a week went by without anyone telling me what was going on. I was feeling much better now and was able to eat solid food. I was going to the bathroom regularly, and the nurses said that was a good sign. I didn't have any more incidents where I was passing out and could walk on my own. I kept asking when I was going to be moved to the hospital ship, but kept getting bullshit answers. I was getting irritated with them, but was told much worse wounded soldiers were being taken out there and that

166

made me feel bad because of my selfishness. The IV was finally removed, and I was given a pass to go into Da Nang. Another Marine and I decided to go into the famous "Dog Patch" (the area we were warned not to go into when I first got there). We got dressed in the new uniforms they gave us and went into town. We caught a pedi-cab outside the gate and headed in on our first adventure to the city.

This place was scary. It was a street lined with bars and massage parlors. We went into several bars and were immediately inundated by the bar girls (hookers) wanting us to buy them a drink they called Saigon Tea. They were very pretty and probably younger than I was. Saigon tea was watered down tea that cost more than a beer. We managed to get away from them. They started calling us things like "cheap Charley" and calling us number ten. Number ten meant we were bad guys. We didn't stay very long in either place. It was crowded with other GI's, smoky, loud, and hot. We decided we would head back to the hospital.

The next day, the same guy and I asked if we could go to the big PX in Da Nang. We were given a pass and told to be back by 1300 hours because the doctor wanted to see me during his rounds that afternoon. Finally, I would find out what had happened to me and be on my way out of country.

We headed to the PX area and found a huge warehouse-looking building. It was like going into Rinks Bargain City (the place I worked prior to joining the Marine Corps). There was a snack bar there and the food smelled great. We decided to have cheeseburgers and french fries. This was the first time I'd eaten that stuff since I left California. It was the best tasting cheeseburger I had ever had. My stomach, however, didn't agree. All the grease made me sick. I headed to the bathroom, where I quickly deposited my lunch in the commode. I told the other guy I had better get back to the hospital because I wasn't feeling so good. He agreed and told me I looked like shit. We both headed on back.

The doctor finally showed up at about 1400 hours. Just like doctors in the states, they were never on time. He asked me what had happened to me because I was looking kind of pale. I told him what I had done, and he said my stomach couldn't handle that kind of food yet (no shit). He said he would look in on me tomorrow and decide what he was going to do with me. I was surprised by that, I thought I was going to go back to the states. They still had not told me what was wrong with me and I was concerned.

The next morning, the nurse came in right after breakfast. She told me I would be released the next day and I could return to my unit. *What,* I thought I was headed home. I asked her what had happened to me. She said I was diagnosed with a disease of unknown origin, and they couldn't do anything for me. I was in shock. I asked her what happened if I got sick again. She said I would probably end up right back in the hospital. I was in total disbelief at what just happened. The Marine I was hanging around with said he was sorry for my situation. I told him it wasn't his fault and wished him well. He was headed home because of his injuries.

The next morning, I was given a ride to the transit station to try to catch a ride back to my home on Hill 37. The doctor had given me a note to take to the battalion surgeon and my company commander that said I was to be on two weeks light duty and not to send me to the field. I finally caught a helicopter ride back to Hill 37. Bock was surprised to see me when I walked into the orderly room. He had been told I was being medevaced back to the states. The company had no idea I was coming back.

The date was around 5 May 1968. I had been in the hospital for almost three weeks. I just wanted to return to my squad and finish my tour.

CHAPTER 12

DEATH OF ANOTHER FRIEND

If you can read this, thank a teacher, If you can read this in English, thank a Marine.

— Unknown Marine

I sensed something was wrong when I was talking to Bock at headquarters upon my return. I asked where the company was, and he said they were on Hill 65. It was an artillery outpost. We could actually see Hill 65 from Hill 37. It got hit a lot. We could sometimes sit on our bunkers on hole watch at night on Hill 37 and watch the fire fights and all the explosions and tracers working on and off that hill when they were in trouble. We were put on reaction force on several occasions to go help when they were about to be overrun. I was always thankful that I was on Hill 37. We were hit almost every night with one thing or another. Sometimes it would be mortars, sometimes rockets or small arms fire, but we experienced nothing like Hill 65 experienced. It was not uncommon for them to have gooks in the wire two or three times a week. Bock told me to go put my gear away in the tent and come back, and we would go to lunch and he would fill me in.

I went into our squad tent and it felt strange. My gear was neatly packed in my sea bag when my squad leader had pulled it from supply because he was told I was going home. I could tell Steve had packed it because it was packed so neatly and orderly. I dug out a fresh uniform, stowed my gear, and took my sea bag back to the supply room to be put back in storage and draw out my M16 rifle. (By the way, my sea bag still smelled like puke.) I met Bock back at headquarters and we went to lunch.

We got our food and sat down in the corner of the tent, away from everyone else. He said, "Tack, I've got some bad news." I just looked at him and thought for sure he was going to tell me I had been assigned to a CAP unit, but it was worse, much worse. He told me Steve was dead. He had been killed on 24 April on Hill 65. It felt like someone had just hit me in the chest with a sledge hammer. I couldn't believe it. I just stared at him. I could feel my eyes tearing up and my chest getting tight. A big lump came up in my throat. I couldn't even drink my water. I was stunned. *Of all people, Steve?* He couldn't be dead. Who the hell was going to keep me squared away and out of trouble? Another one of my friends was dead. How in the hell could I take much more of this shit?

I asked Bock what had happened. He said, a couple of days before Steve was killed, Hill 65 had got hit hard, very hard. They were almost overrun and they had a lot of casualties. They sent Kilo Company to the hill to help secure it until another unit could be assigned to it and to help clean it up. There were unexploded dud rounds everywhere. Bock explained that this is where everything gets fuzzy about what happened.

There are four versions of how Steve died. I will tell all four versions, since I wasn't there to witness it first hand, and I want to write this as truthfully as I can. I believe it's only right to tell everyone's story. The first, the official Marine

Corps version, only states that it was, "Non-hostile, died of other causes." How in the hell could it be non-hostile? How do you explain that to his family? I didn't find that out until 2001, when I was looking on the Vietnam Memorial Wall website to find his name. It states: Non-hostile, died of other causes.

The second version, the one Bock told me in May 1968, went something like this. After the company arrived at Hill 65, the commander divided the company into different areas of the hill. The combat engineers had established a collection point for all of the unexploded ordinance. If we found something, we were to carefully take it to the pit the engineers dug and gently place it in the pit and move out. Rock's team was short one man: me. They were given two bunkers to clear. Bobby and Steve were in one bunker; Rock and Mike R. in the other. Bock said the report they got at headquarters was that Steve was in a bunker clearing it when he called out to Bobby that he had found an unexploded hand grenade. Bobby was pulling security on top of the bunker. Bobby said, "Okay, bring it out," when—*boom*—the grenade went off killing Steve instantly. That was the report the company turned in to higher headquarters.

The third version I heard from Bobby himself. I did not see Bobby again until 2002 at a Kilo Third of the Seventh reunion in Louisville, Kentucky. Bobby was severely wounded and almost died in late May 1968, while on Operation Allen Brook in the Arizona Territory. Bobby, his wife, and I were having a quiet drink in the bar one evening when the subject of Steve came up. Bobby's version is the version I believe, and explains why the Marine Corps deemed it a non-hostile fatality. The first part was exactly as Bock explained. Bobby and Steve were clearing a bunker, and he was on security on top of the bunker. Bobby then told me that a couple of days before they went to Hill 65 for the cleanup, Steve got a "Dear John" letter from his girlfriend. She broke up with him for another guy. I know Steve must have been devastated. That girl was all Steve talked about. He was deeply in love. She was his high school sweetheart, and they were going to get married when he got out of the Marine Corps. Bobby said Steve went into a deep, deep funk. He wouldn't talk to anybody, he would barely eat, and he was just not the same happy guy we all knew. I certainly can understand what he was going through.

Bobby said Steve insisted on going into the bunker alone to clear it. Bobby said he looked in and didn't see any unexploded ordinance, but it still had to be checked out, so he told Steve to go ahead. Bobby climbed on top of the bunker and Steve went in. Suddenly, BOOM, a grenade went off, killing Steve instantly. Bobby jumped off the bunker and jumped in only to find Steve's body a mangled mess. His right hand was gone and his head was nearly blown off. Bobby said he thinks Steve pulled a pin on one of his own hand grenades and let it blow up in his face. I couldn't believe what I was hearing. I do believe if anyone would do something like that over a girl, it would be Steve. He was that much in love and he couldn't take the pain of losing her.

At this point, both of us were in tears. Bobby's wife had to get up and leave the table. Bobby and I hugged and cried. He said that was the first time he had told anyone that story since Steve died in 1968 in that damn bunker. I felt so bad that I wasn't there for Steve. I can't help but think that, had I been there, things might have been different. I could have comforted him when he got the Dear John and helped him through his pain. I could have talked to him and assured him there was no girl in the world worth doing something stupid for. Nobody knows what might have happened if I would have been there, but I would like to think I could have made a difference. Steve was one of my best friends in Vietnam, and he was dead, and there was nothing I could do about it.

The fourth version, and the most unbelievable version, came up at a Kilo Third of the Seventh reunion in 2009, in Colorado Springs. I was sitting in the hospitality suite when Bobby came up to me and introduced me to a guy who said he was in our squad during that time. Bobby was tired and had to go to take a nap, so the guy and I sat and talked. I didn't remember him. He had gotten to the squad when I was still in the hospital in Da Nang. He was only in the squad a short time and was wounded and moved back to the states in May during the same operation that Bobby was wounded on. This guy was in our squad, but in the other fire team.

His version went like this. He said they were sent to Hill 65 after it had almost gotten overrun. He hadn't been there but a couple of days at that point and didn't know anybody very well, but remembered Bobby, Steve, and a guy named Sims,. He said Sims, Steve, and he were at the bunker that night on hole watch after they had cleared it. They started receiving small arms fire on their side of the perimeter and dove into the bunker for protection. He said an automatic weapon opened up on the bunker and hit Steve and Sims, killing them both.

That didn't jive with any other accounts of what happened, but I didn't pursue it with him any further. I told him Steve's death was considered a non-hostile fatality, and he was pissed. He said we had to do something about it, and he was going to write a letter to the commandant of the Marine Corps when he got back home. I know combat does strange things to a person, but I had no idea it could cause a complete delusion. I avoided the guy the rest of the reunion.

I wrestled with the question of if I should tell Bobby what he had said. I finally decided I would talk to Bobby about how well he knew the guy. As Bobby and I were talking, I gently broached the subject of Steve again. I asked Bobby how well he knew the guy from the reunion. He said he didn't really know him because he was in the other fire team in our squad. I decided I would tell Bobby what he said, and he was astounded by what I told him. He assured me it happened the way that he had told me, and I told Bobby I 100 percent believed him and thought we should keep our distance from that guy. I knew Bobby would blow a gasket on this guy, so we stayed away from him for the remaining two days of the reunion. The guy has never come to another reunion.

I have always felt bad about what happened to Steve. Steve is buried in a small cemetery in his hometown in Missouri. Steve was only nineteen years old. One of my missions is to go and visit Steve's grave site and place a Purple Heart on his gravestone. I will also place a picture of him and me there and hope that, wherever he may be, he's at peace.

This chapter is dedicated to my friend

Lance Corporal Steve Davis

United States Marine Corps.

LANCE CORPORAL STEVE DAVIS

KILO COMPANY

THIRD BATTALION

SEVENTH MARINE REGIMENT

BORN: 18 OCTOBER 1948

KILLED IN ACTION: 24 APRIL 1968 HILL 65, VIETNAM

STEVE DAVIS's NAME IS ON
THE VIETNAM MEMORIAL WALL AT

PANEL 51E

LINE 045

WELCOME HOME, STEVE

April 1968
Left to Right: Donald, Bobbie, Flores, Steve (KIA – Apr. 1968)

Mike R., Steve, Bankenship, Rock
Chicken Man

Pvt. Donald G. Tackett

Pvt. Donald G. Tackett
Hill 37

Bobby – R&R Bangkok

Donald & Rock

Lance Cpl Donald G. Tackett, son of Mrs. Frank Ferry of 1022 Sunset avenue, is serving with the Third Battalion, Seventh Marine Regiment in Vietnam.

As a member of the battalion he helps capture or destroy enemy forces. He accomplished his through weapons fire, tactical maneuvering, and both large and small scale operations.

June 19, 1968

Hometown News Release

CHAPTER 13
THE BOYS FROM ZANESVILLE

I wanna go home.

> – Benjamin Buford (Bubba) Blue
> From the movie, *FORREST GUMP*

I have decided to break from the routine of the story to tell you about the boys from my home town, Zanesville, Ohio, that I met while in Vietnam. First, let me tell you a little about Zanesville. The population back in 1967 was somewhere around 35,000, I think. Not a large community. While I was in Vietnam, I came upon three other guys from Zanesville. One was two years older than me, and graduated with my oldest brother Frank. One was one year older than me, and graduated with my brother Dave. The last one was my age and graduated with me. All three were United States Marines. It was very much a coincidence that I would run into these three guys in a country so far away from Zanesville, Ohio.

The first guy I ran into was actually assigned to the same battalion that I was, except he was in Headquarters Company. His name was Ron Brock. He knew and graduated with my oldest brother, Frank. Ron was on his second tour of duty in Vietnam. His MOS was truck driver. After we met, every time I had to go to Da Nang, I would find Ron to see if he could drive me. We had some very interesting adventures, to say the least.

I met Ron one evening around 2100 hours. I was in my tent writing a letter when I heard the unmistakable sound of 122 mm rockets heading our way. We could tell they were coming and had a few seconds to react before they hit. They sounded like freight trains. I heard the sound, threw down my writing pad, and jumped out the door of our tent and into our bunker. The first two rockets hit doing little damage. Everyone ran back into the tent, grabbed their gear and headed for the perimeter. The most likely time for the enemy to attack was as soon as rockets or mortars exploded. I headed to the nearest bunker on the perimeter and dove in head first as mortar rounds starting going off inside the perimeter. I landed right on top of some guy who started yelling and cussing for me to get off of him. We both looked out the portals of the bunker expecting an attack at any time. No attack came, so we relaxed.

We started talking, just the usual small talk two guys make when they don't know each other. He said his name was Ron, and he had just gotten to Hill 37 about a week before. He told me this was his second tour and he was a truck driver. I asked him where he was from in the world and he said he was from a little town in Ohio that I probably never heard of. I told him I was from Ohio too, and asked what town was he from. He said, Zanesville. I nearly hit the roof with excitement.

I said, "Hey, that's where I'm from!"

He thought I was kidding him, but I told him what street I lived on and, wouldn't you know it, he lived about three blocks from me. Wow, I was excited. I had been in Vietnam for about nine months by that time and wanted to hear all about good old Zanesville. I forgot all about the fact he had been in the Marine Corps for the past three years and had only been home on leave. That didn't matter to me. I just wanted to hear about home.

He graduated in 1965, and he knew my oldest brother Frank. They weren't good friends, but they knew each other. That was great. Of all places to meet someone from my hometown, in a bunker, during a mortar and rocket attack, in a foreign country. I just happened to jump in the bunker he was pulling hole watch in. The all clear was given, but instead of going back to my tent to go to bed, I sat and talked with him until about one o'clock in the morning. I told him I would catch up with him in the next couple of days and we would talk.

The next time we saw each other was in the mess tent eating dinner one night. I told him I had a trip to Da Nang the next day, so he arranged to drive me. It became a common occurrence during my last three months in country.

On one of the trips, I and a couple of other guys from Kilo Company got a pass and decided to go into the big PX in Da Nang. Ron drove us. Just before we got to Da Nang, which was about twenty-five miles away, Ron pulled off at this small village to drop off his laundry. He said the Mamasan inside was always trying to get him to sell her sodas and cigarettes, so she could sell them to GI's that stopped there on the black market. I told Ron we should teach her a lesson. We got the Mamasan to agree to pay us ten dollars each for a case of sodas, and five dollars each for one carton of cigarettes. She wanted ten cases of sodas and ten cartons of cigarettes. It would only cost us about thirty bucks for all of that, and she would have to pay us $150.00 when we returned.

We went on into Da Nang, and I told my two friends from Kilo that I had no intentions of giving her the sodas or cigarettes. We would try and rip her off. They agreed. I did not make Ron aware of our plan because he stopped there all the time to get his laundry done.

We got the stuff at the PX and headed back to the hill. I had Mike sit in the front of the truck with Ron, while Dave and I sat in the back with the loot. I told Mike, to tell Ron to stay in the truck and to keep the motor running while I made the deal with Mamasan. We pulled up to the hootch and Mamasan came out. I lifted the cover on the sodas and showed her the cartons of cigarettes. She wanted us to unload it, but I told her no, that I wanted to see her money first. She held out the $150.00 in military payment certificates (MPC) and I grabbed it out of her hand and started yelling for Ron to, "Go, go, go." He stepped on the gas not knowing what was going on. Mamasan was yelling at us and her husband, who was an ARVN, came out with his carbine. Dave and I fired off a couple of M16 rounds over their heads to run them off. They dove into a ditch. That was the last time I saw Mamasan. We laughed all the way back to the hill. Even though I feel bad about it today, I didn't give it a second thought then.

When we got back to Hill 37, Ron didn't know what was going on. I told him I ripped off Mamasan and he would have to find another place to get his laundry done. I divided up the money and sodas between the four of us and gave Ron my share of the cigarettes since I didn't smoke. Ron was pissed at me for a couple of days, but got over it. We finally had a good laugh about it.

I know you might be saying how wrong it was for me to rip off the Mamasan. First, she was probably a Viet Cong. Second, she was making five or ten times the amount of money she would have paid us for the stuff on the black market. I didn't feel bad at all. Ron had to alter his routes, however, when returning to Da Nang.

I met up with Ron when we both got out of the Marine Corps a couple of years later. We had a great time hanging out in the bars and telling our war stories to each other. Ron was a good friend and still lives somewhere around Zanesville today.

The second Zanesvillian I will talk about graduated with my brother Dave. I will call him Kent because I cannot confirm the stories I am about to tell. But I have a very strong suspicion they are true. I got a letter from my mother one day asking me if I remembered Kent from school. I thought, *yes, he went to school with Dave*. I had heard he had gone AWOL from the Marines, or at least that was what I was told. My mom knew his mom. My mom worked in a jewelry store downtown. People would come in and pay their utility bills there, so she pretty much knew everyone. Anyway, she told me that Kent was in Vietnam. She told me what unit he was in and that he was on Hill 10. I knew exactly where Hill 10 was. It was not far from Hill 37.

I made arrangements for Ron to drive me to Da Nang on one of my missions. Hill 10 was right along the way. The problem was we would also have to drive past the Mamasan's hootch we had ripped off earlier. I told Ron we would just have to haul ass past her hootch. And if she came out, I would just have to shoot her if she started any shit or tried to stop us. He said okay. We stopped at Hill 10 to find Kent and found him in the main commo bunker, where he was a communications radio operator. We had lunch with him and talked a lot about Zanesville. He hadn't been in Vietnam very long. I asked him if he went AWOL, and Kent said he had extended his leave himself and was picked up by the city police and put back into Marine Corps custody. He said he was picked up at the high school, which was embarrassing, where he was visiting friends. Kent never confirmed he was AWOL, but I knew what he meant.

I asked him if he had seen any field duty. He said no, he was just a commo guy and spent most of his time in the commo bunker on radio watch or on hole watch. I found it strange that the only thing Kent wanted to know about me was how many gooks I had killed. I didn't really have a response to the question. I told him we would have to arrange a time when he could go into Da Nang with Ron and me, and he said he would try. We went on our way. We saw him a couple of more times. The last trip to Hill 10, Ron and I went into the commo bunker to find him, and we met up with his team sergeant. I asked Kent's sergeant where he was, and the sergeant started cussing Kent, calling him a coward and all kinds of names. I asked what the problem was, and he told me Kent had shot himself in the foot to get out of country. I never saw Kent again.

Some years later, I started going to my high school reunions. One guy came up to me, and we were talking about my time in Vietnam. He mentioned he knew Kent had been in Vietnam, also.

I said, "Yes, I saw him while I was there. Our units were not very far apart from each other and I could go see him on occasion."

About an hour later, the same guy came up to me with a couple other guys and asked if it was true that Kent shot himself in the foot. I told them, I was told by his team sergeant that he had, but I didn't know because I didn't see him do it. I believed his Sergeant. I asked them what Kent had told them. They said Kent told them he had been wounded and was sent home and discharged. I didn't comment either way.

In 2004, my mother passed away. After her memorial service, a bunch of us were standing around talking. Another guy I grew up with started talking about Kent, who was a good friend of his. He asked me directly if it was true that Kent had shot himself. I told him what Kent's Sergeant had told me, and that I suspected he had. I've never talked to Kent about this; in fact, I have never seen him again. I know he still lives in Zanesville. Whatever happened to Kent in Vietnam is between Kent and the United States Marine Corps as far as I'm concerned.

The last guy I saw was a guy I graduated with. His name was Bobby Garrett. I had known Bobby for quite a few years before entering the Marine Corps. I didn't know Bobby had enlisted.

Sometime around July or August 1968, our company had a lot of casualties in the hospital in Da Nang. I had the mission to take them some things before they were to be shipped back to the states to recover from their wounds. A few of us took off for Da Nang for the visit. We found the ward our guys were in and, while walking down the rows of wounded, I heard someone calling my name. I thought it was one of our guys, but it wasn't. It was Bobby Garrett. What a surprise. We talked for awhile, and I asked him what had happened. He told me that his squad and another squad were on a night patrol when they ran into each other by accident. One of the patrols had gotten lost. They both started shooting at each other, and he was wounded. He wasn't wounded seriously and would return to his unit. Bobby was assigned to Second Battalion, First Marines. I had no idea where they were, or if I would ever see him again.

I had to cut short our visit, but promised to stay in contact with him. But I never heard from him after that. In late October, I was reading *The Stars and Stripes* (a military newspaper about what was happening in all the services, as well as news from back home), there is always a section devoted to the weeks service members Killed in Action. Their names, units, and date they were killed were published. Much to my surprise and dismay, there was Bobby's name. He had been killed on 22 October 1968 by some sort of explosive device. I was devastated.

Bobby's name is on the Vietnam Memorial wall in Washington DC as well as on a memorial in Zanesville. .

Welcome home, Bobby

It's hard to imagine being so far away from home and not being with anyone you know. You have to form new friendships and bonds. When you do run into someone from your hometown, it becomes one big reunion—especially if your only eighteen or nineteen years old and have never been away from home before.

Welcome home, boys from Zanesville

CHAPTER 14

BACK TO THE WAR:

OPERATION ALLEN BROOK

We're not retreating. Hell, we're just attacking in another direction.

— General Oliver Smith, USMC

Things were getting somewhat back to normal. With the loss of Steve, I was also lost. What was I going to do? It became harder and harder to make friends for fear they would be the next to die. The company was still on Hill 65 doing cleanup. Bock noticed I was just not the same. As we were eating one evening, he asked me if I would like to take an R&R. I told him I wasn't due for one for at least two more months, but he told me the company had one quota for Hong Kong that nobody wanted. He talked to the first sergeant. Since I was still recovering, the first sergeant said I could have it if I wanted it. I was to pack up and leave in two days for my five days in heaven. The company was not due back from Hill 65 for at least five days, so I took it.

A Marine can play the time-frame game of R&R if he knows the system. I would leave on the morning mail run to Da Nang and fly out the next day to Hong Kong. When I arrived back from R&R I could push it for two more days in Da Nang saying I couldn't catch a ride back to the hill. R&R could last up to nine days if a person played his cards right. The key is not to push your luck. Everybody knew the game and how it was played. Some did take advantage of the situation, however, and got themselves in a lot of trouble.

I had to go to Hill 55 to draw my money out of finance. We had to travel down the dreaded Liberty Road. I didn't have a weapon, and that made me nervous, so I held the driver's weapon. We made it without incident, which made all of us in the vehicle very happy, especially since I had to turn in my weapon before going on R&R. We could keep our money on the books and not draw all our pay at once and save some for things like R&R. I only drew twenty-five dollars a month cash, so I had plenty of money to spend in Hong Kong. One of the things I wanted to do most was buy two nice, fitted suits. Hong Kong was famous for their tailors and their fine fabrics.

I met up with another Marine in Da Nang as we processed for our flight to Hong Kong. We decided to hang out together. We were always told to go out with a crowd or at least two together. If a person was alone, the more likely they would be robbed or even murdered, so it sounded like a plan to me. That night in Da Nang, we decided to go to the steam baths to try to sweat out some of the dirt in our bodies and get nice haircuts. My only thought was getting clean. I had been clean while I was in the hospital, but I felt a good steam bath would do me some good.

We found one close to the main gate and went in. I had never been in a steam bath before and was surprised to find out I could actually get a haircut, steam bath, and a massage for little money. I think we paid five or ten dollars for all three. That was just the hook. When the young lady had you on the massage table after the haircut and steam bath, that's where the real negotiations began.

For extra money, she would perform whatever sex act you preferred as long as you paid her. I wasn't interested; I just wanted to get the hell out of there. My buddy, on the other hand, had other thoughts. I waited outside for about thirty minutes and started getting nervous, so I went back to the tent we had been assigned. A couple hours later, my buddy came in. He was almost broke. He had spent most of his money in the steam bath. He didn't have enough money to go to Hong Kong. I told him I would lend him a hundred bucks, and I would pay for the hotel room in Hong Kong that we *were* going to share and split the cost. He said he would pay me back when we got back.

The trip to Hong Kong came and went. The next thing I knew I was almost broke, had two brand new suits (one made of shark skin and one pin stripe) and was trying to find a ride back to Hill 37. My buddy ditched me when we got to the hotel in Hong Kong, and I didn't see him again until we were on the plane back to Da Nang. We exchanged addresses so he could send me my money. I never heard from him again. I never really expected I would.

I finally got a ride to the hill and was ready for some sleep when I got there. I was still on light duty, so I knew I wouldn't be sent out to the field anytime soon. When I arrived, I reported in to Bock at the orderly room. He told me I had just missed Bobby. Bobby had gotten his R&R and was headed for Bangkok, Thailand. He would be back in about nine days or so. Bock said if I had waited, I would have been able to go to Bangkok with Bobby. I know I would have had a good time with Bobby. He was the closest friend I had left.

Finally, my light duty was over. Rock was glad to have me back in the team. Since I was on light duty and Bobby was on R&R, he was short two men in his team. Rock told me to go to supply and draw out my weapon; we had a briefing in about an hour. When I went to supply, I found out they were issuing us the new M16A2 rifle. The Old M16A1s they had issued us had problems jamming in a fire fight after a number of rounds were fired. I didn't have that problem because I still had my M14. The supply Sergeant told me I couldn't have my M14 back and, I would have the new M16A2. I was not a happy Marine. I went back to the tent and told Rock they wouldn't give me my M14 back. He was pissed but knew there wasn't anything that could be done. Rock told me to start cleaning my new rifle because we were going on a mission the next morning.

Our mission the next morning was to escort the engineers down Liberty Road to Hill 55 on a road sweep operation. *Here we go again*, I thought. I hated that damned road. I cleaned my new M16 really good. I had it oiled, performed the functions check, and was ready to go. I was supposed to be given time to test fire it, but there was no time left. I would have to hope it worked.

We left the gate onto Liberty Road just after first light. We were out about an hour when we came up to the famous dog-leg in the road. Sure enough, the Viet Cong ambushed us. They hit us hard with automatic weapons and RPG's. We dove for cover on the left side of the road and returned fire into the tree line on our right. It was a fierce fire fight for about the first thirty minutes. Rounds were pinging off the road in front of me as I shot back.

Suddenly, my weapon jammed. I had fired about two or three magazines, and it jammed. I couldn't get the charging handle to budge and eject the casing in the chamber. It was frozen. Rock kept hollering at me to keep firing, but I told him my weapon was jammed. He yelled for me to crawl behind the big rock to our rear and clear it. I did my best low crawl, watching rounds hit the rock and hoping I didn't get hit by a ricochet. I couldn't pull the pin to break the weapon down until I cleared it, so I was sitting behind that big rock with rounds hitting all around me kicking the charging handle to free it up.

Finally, it broke free, and I was able to clear the weapon. I had the whole weapon torn apart when the firing started to ease up. A pair of helicopter gunships had shown up on the scene and were firing on the tree line to stop the ambush. I finally got my weapon put back together and fired a couple extra magazines into the tree line for good measure.

Nobody was injured, but we were sent into the tree line to see if there were any dead bodies of the VC there. My nerves were on end by now, and I hoped if we got into another fire fight my weapon wouldn't jam again. We moved about a hundred meters into the tree line, but only found some blood trails and some dropped equipment. We went back to the road and finished the road sweep.

The trip back to Hill 37 was uneventful. We caught a ride on a two and a half ton truck, so we didn't have to walk back. It wasn't even noon time, and I was worn out already. I guess I hadn't fully recovered from my disease of unknown origin.

I was able to take a nap, but my sound sleep was interrupted by Rock telling me our team had hole watch that night. I would have to get used to sleepless nights again. We were assigned our positions. Rock and I were in one bunker, and the other two guys in our team were in the other. Neither of us was tired so we were talking, I asked Rock what the future held for us. He said the company was going on a major operation called Operation Allen Brook. Rock said Operation Allen Brook would take us back into the Arizona Territory. We would be attacking a known North Vietnamese Regiment in an area called Ga Noi Island. This was a bad place. I had heard of it before and knew it was very dangerous. The operation would involve three or four battalions of Marines. An operation this size could go on for months.

We moved out for Operation Allen Brook two days later without Bobby. He was still on R&R. We headed down Liberty Road to Liberty Bridge. I hated that place and was glad we were only there for one night. We crossed over into the Arizona that night and Operation Allen Brook began. Contact with the enemy was light the first couple of days. The weather was extremely hot. It was at least 110 degrees every day with very high humidity. I wasn't feeling very well and Rock could see it in my face.

I passed out on day four and I woke up with an IV in my arm. I was told I was going to be medevaced as soon as a helicopter could be cut loose. Another Marine battalion was taking heavy casualties and needed all the medevacs they could get their hands on. I started feeling better and told Rock and our corpsman I would be okay. The corpsman kept the IV in my arm for about an hour, then removed it. I continued on for a couple more hours. I was one sick Marine again, and Rock could see it. A resupply helicopter came in that afternoon. Rock and the corpsman had me put on the helicopter to go back to the Battalion Aide Station. I didn't realize how damn sick I was until I got back to the aid station. My temperature was 103 degrees. I was burning up. I was having a relapse of my disease of unknown origin.

Bock came into the aide station to see me. He told me Bobby had gotten back from R&R and found out I had been medevaced and left two pictures for me from his R&R. I still have those pictures to this day in my photo album from Vietnam. I had missed Bobby again. He flew out to the company right after he got back. The next day I was feeling much better. I got out of the aide station to try to get back to the field. Bock told me I was to stay in the rear area for at least three days to recover. I felt bad that I couldn't rejoin my team. I knew this was a major operation, and I wanted to be a part of it.

The next morning, Bock asked me if I wanted to be a POW escort. They had three POW's at Liberty Bridge and needed escorts to bring them back to Hill 37. I grabbed my gear and headed out down Liberty Road. There was another Marine with me on the back of the truck to assist. We got to Liberty Bridge to pick up the three POW's, they looked younger than I did. They didn't look to be any older than fourteen years old. I was still eighteen years old. Their hands were tied behind their backs and they were sitting on the ground. They looked scared to death.

We had to wait for awhile before we took them back to Hill 37, so the other Marine and I sat in the shade waiting. I started talking to him and asked him what his job was in the battalion. He said he worked in the S-1 in Headquarters Company as the awards clerk. He typed up all the award recommendations when they were submitted by the different companies in the battalion and was tired of not being able to get in the shit. He had been in Vietnam for longer than nine months and wanted some trigger time. I guess he saw all the awards being given and thought he could get one himself. Whatever the case, he was sadly mistaken if he thought getting an award was glorious.

He said he had never been to the field and in nine months had never fired his weapon. I told him it wasn't all that it was cracked up to be and it wasn't like in the movies. He had this look of hatred on his face. I guess he was pissed because he couldn't get ice in his coke in the rear or something. He just stared at the POW's.

He said he would like to blow one of them mother fuckers away. I was worried that this John-Wayne-wannabe would do something stupid. The problem was he was a corporal, and I was just a lance corporal. He was in charge.

We got the okay to load up the POW's on the truck. We were given sand bags to cover their faces. We put the sand bags over their heads and drew the draw strings tight so the bags wouldn't blow off while going down the road. The corporal decided he would tighten his sand bag so tight around the POW's neck that the POW started choking. I told him to loosen the sand bag, but he just stared at me and told me to mind my own fucking business.

This was not going to end well for one of us. I went to the tent where we reported and told the NCO what had just happened. He came out of the tent and ordered the corporal to loosen the bag—we needed the POW's alive. The corporal got pissed at me, but I didn't care. I wasn't there to be his buddy, I was there for a mission and I was going to accomplish it. I wasn't going to be a part of a murder.

As we drove out of the gate of Liberty Bridge onto Liberty Road, the corporal looked at me and said if we got ambushed on the way back, he was going to shoot one of the fucking gook POW's and I had better not try to stop him. I told him if he did, I would report his ass. I was a seasoned field Marine by that time and I wasn't about to let this idiot murder a prisoner just for the sake of writing up his own award. Luck was on my side and the side of the POWs. We made it back to Hill 37 without incident. As we entered the gate, the corporal got irate and started cussing and hitting one of the POWs with the butt of his rifle. I grabbed him and pushed him down on the bed of the truck and told him to knock that shit off. I got between him and the POW until we got back to the Intelligence tent. The intelligence sergeant came out of the tent to retrieve the POWs and I didn't say anything about what had happened earlier.

The POW's still had the sand bags over their faces and their hands were still tied behind their backs. I grabbed the first POW and lifted him up to help him off the back of the truck. The intel sergeant helped the POW down. An officer also came out of the tent along with a Vietnamese interpreter. The corporal grabbed the second POW and almost lifted him clear off the ground. His feet were barely touching the bed of the truck. I was helping the third POW when I saw the corporal throw the POW off the side of the truck. The POW landed on his head and neck. He was hurt bad. The intel sergeant started yelling at the corporal and ordered someone to get a corpsman and a litter.

I grabbed the corporal and threw him down on the bed of the truck. I was pissed and had enough of his bullshit. I was on top of him and about to start beating his ass when the officer told me to let him go. I helped the last POW off the truck and jumped down. The intel sergeant told me to go in the tent and write a statement of what had happened. I told him of the other things that happened earlier, he told me to put those things in my statement, also.

I couldn't believe how the corporal acted. Just because he had never been to the field did not give him any excuse to act the way he did. He was a clerk, not a grunt; not even the grunts I knew would act like that. I finished my statement and the intel sergeant thanked me and told me to return to my unit. I asked him what was going to happen to the corporal and he said not to worry, he would be taken care of. Hill 37 was a small hill and I knew I would be seeing the corporal again. I hoped I would see him somewhere where I could teach him a lesson. I wanted to beat his ass.

I went back to our orderly room to tell Bock I was back and to tell him what had happened. Bock said he knew the corporal very well and that the guy was a complete ass. He was glad the corporal was going to get his ass handed to him. I had the rest of the day off and decided I would write some letters. I hadn't gotten much mail lately, especially from my girlfriend and was wondering what was going on.

That evening Bock and I were in the mess tent eating when we saw the corporal come in from the POW detail. He saw us sitting and eating and came up to us wanting to join us at our table. I couldn't believe the nerve of the guy. He said the commander had told him to write up a letter of appreciation for me for the POW detail and he needed my name and company. I gave him my name and company and told him I already had one Purple Heart and had been put in for a Bronze Star with "V" device, so it shouldn't be hard to find my file. Bock started laughing. The corporal just stared at me and didn't know what to say. I told the corporal what he did that day was fucked up and I hope he got what he deserved. He was pissed; he got up and left the table. I told Bock, I just told the corporal that because I wanted to piss him off. It worked. Bock told me the corporal had been suspected of writing up awards for himself and his buddies in the rear. They just hadn't caught him.

A couple of days went by with me spending a lot of time at the battalion aide station. I was feeling sick again and all they could do was put IV's in my arm. Operation Allen Brook was moving along at a brisk pace. The infantry battalions were seeing a lot of action and there were a lot of casualties. Kilo Company had five killed in action at that point and about thirty-eight wounded. It was tough going, and I was missing it.

I knew a lot of the guys that were wounded and one of the KIA's. The one KIA I knew had a wife and a new baby. His baby had been born just after he arrived in Vietnam. He never got to see his little girl. I felt really bad for him and his family. They brought his body into the battalion aide station for final identification. I went with Bock to identify him. They unzipped the body bag, he had been shot directly in the throat by a sniper. I will never forget the look on his face. His eyes and mouth were wide open as if to say, "I can't believe I was just shot."

I was shook up and needed to get drunk really bad. I was released from the aide station that afternoon and went to find Bock to see if he wanted to get drunk. He knew I was messed up and agreed, but wanted to show me something first. He said it would make me feel better. I didn't know how that could be possible. We walked out to the back of the latrines, and there he was: the corporal that had to go before his company commander for office hours for his actions with the POW's. He was busted to private and was on the shit burning detail. The look on his face was priceless. He saw me standing there grinning and just looked down and continued to burn shit. I never did get the letter of appreciation the idiot corporal (I mean *private*) told me I was supposed to get, but that was okay. Just watching him burn shit was appreciation enough for me. I found out later the POW he threw off the truck broke his neck in the fall and didn't make it. To my knowledge, the corporal, I mean private, was never charged with killing the POW.

A couple of days later, I was on detail helping the supply sergeant when Bock came running into the supply room. He told me Bobby had been seriously wounded and had been medevaced into Da Nang. I got released from the supply detail and hauled ass to try to find a ride into Da Nang to the hospital. I found out later Bobby had stepped on a land mine and was badly injured. He couldn't be medevaced until the next day and almost died that night in our squad leader's arms. I had to get in to see him.

I caught the mail run in the next day to the hospital. I went straight to the NSA hospital where he was taken. I was too late. His injuries were so bad, they had already shipped him out to Japan. The nurse said he wasn't in very good shape and didn't know if he would make it. Bobby did make it. He spent more than a year in the hospital recovering from his wounds. We met up at a Kilo Third of the Seventh reunion in 2002. Bobby is partially paralyzed on his right side from his wounds.

Another friend had been seriously wounded and almost died, and I wasn't there for him. This damn war was taking a toll on my young eighteen-year-old ass.

Operation Allen Brook ended for Kilo Third of the Seventh in late May, 1968. There were around 3,000 Marines from the Seventh Marine Regiment that participated in Operation Allen Brook. The casualty figures for the entire Seventh Marine Regiment, which included First Battalion, Second Battalion, and Third Battalion, totaled eighty-five killed in action, and 859 wounded in action. This operation included some of the bloodiest fighting during the Vietnam War for the Seventh Marines.

Donald and Bobby in 2012
at the Oklahoma City Kilo 3/7 reunion

CHAPTER 15

28 JULY, 1968:

DEATH IN DODGE CITY

I've always been proud of being a United States Marine. I won't hesitate to defend the Corps.

— Jonathan Winters, comic and Marine

There is certainly nothing funny about being a United States Marine fighting for your country. The famous comedian Jonathan Winters was a Marine. He made no bones about the fact that he would fight for the honor of the Corps with his very last breath. I heard him once give a very emotional speech about his time with, and love for, the Corps. It was inspirational to say the least. Mr. Winters enlisted in the Marine Corps at the age of seventeen. He served two years in the Pacific during World War II.

Most of my time in the month of June 1968 was spent in and out of the hospital with my disease of unknown origin. The doctors still did not know what was causing me to display malaria-like symptoms, but were determined to keep me in country and in my company. This didn't fly too well with some of the guys in third platoon. I heard one guy say I was shamming; a term used for someone who was always getting out of going to the bush without anything being wrong with him. I wished that guy could have experienced some of the fainting spells, high temperatures, nausea, diarrhea, and low blood pressure I was experiencing.

I was kept back at Hill 37, where I was put on details that would not cause a lot of stress. Of course, I felt bad about it, but I couldn't do a thing about it. I was sick, and didn't know why. To get me out of the area, Bock got me assigned to convoy duty. I would be a guard on trucks that had to make runs into Da Nang every now and then. I liked that because we would always stop at the big PX in Da Nang and get pogey bait (snacks and comfort food) and really good cheeseburgers, when my stomach could handle it. We would sometimes get to catch a USO show that was playing there. It was great duty, but I wanted to be in the bush with my squad. I managed to go out several times on small patrols and ambushes, but I was not allowed to go out on extended operations. Rock was okay with that and said I was a good Marine and he would welcome me back anytime I wanted to and was able to. That made me feel good.

July 1968 came by with yet another month of illness for me. I was about to spend my nineteenth birthday in the hospital. I had been sick for about a week and had been transferred again to the NSA hospital in Da Nang. There would be no birthday cake. I was too sick to eat it anyway. I was on IV's again and a liquid diet.

I remember the doctor coming in and saying, "I don't know what I'm going to do with you, young man." Hell, if he didn't know, who did?

I finally went back to Hill 37 around the middle of July. I reported to the orderly room and Bock had some disturbing news for me. The first sergeant told him to send me to Headquarters Company for temporary duty. The first sergeant didn't want me hanging around the company doing nothing. When it came to sympathy, there was little to pass around.

The first sergeant said not to come back until I was cleared by the doctors for full duty. I was upset, but kind of relieved. I wouldn't be going back to the bush anytime soon. I would definitely miss my squad, but I understood where the first sergeant was coming from. I would have rather stayed in Kilo Company working in the supply room or orderly room, but I was holding up a slot that could be filled by someone healthy.

I reported to Headquarters Company and back to the S-1. Bill, the guy I came to Hill 37 with way back in December 1967, was still there. He had replaced the awards clerk I talked about previously, who got in trouble for writing out his own awards and killing the POW. The old awards clerk was sent to a CAP unit. Sam told me I was being assigned to the mail room for the time being. He said if I wanted, he would try to make it permanent. I told him that would be great, but I knew it probably was not going to happen. It was not my luck. I was still sick, but could work there with no problem. On the positive side, the mail room was near the latrine, and I still had a bad case of diarrhea.

I walked back to my old squad tent to tell Rock what was going on. The squad had just returned from patrol. There were three new guys in the squad I had never seen. One of them was my replacement. Rock was happy for me and told me I moved just in time. The company was about to move out on another major operation out in Arizona Territory; they would be going into the area we called Dodge City. It was a bad place to be. I told him I would be back in the company as soon as I got better, but he told me not to hurry. If I could stay there, do it. I thanked him for everything he had done for me and told him if there was anything I could do for him to let me know. Little did I know, that would be the last time I ever saw or talked to him.

I started my new duties making the mail runs into Da Nang every day. We took the same route every time we went in and I didn't think that was too smart. My infantry training was catching up to me. The squad never had a set routine when moving in the bush. The enemy will take advantage of that and set an ambush. On my third trip into Da Nang, we were following a big two and half ton truck. The road was dusty, we laid back a ways so as not to have to eat so much dust. There seemed to be a lot of traffic that day on the road. Civilians were everywhere. At a bend in the road, I could see the truck following very closely to a man and woman on a small Honda motorcycle. It was not uncommon to see these small Hondas loaded down with all kind of stuff traveling the roads. All of a sudden, the truck hit the motor cycle and bodies went flying everywhere. The truck ran over the woman and just kept going. The man driving the motorcycle jumped off just at the right time and was uninjured.

I yelled at my driver to stop to see if there was anything we could do. There was a lot of commotion and yelling from the people on the side of the road. The man got up and started yelling at us. There was nothing we could do for the woman. She was dead. The thing I found strange was the man wasn't concerned about the dead woman; he was concerned about his crushed motorcycle. The crowd began to get angrier and very aggressive, so the driver and I pulled the woman's body off to the side of the road and left her there. We didn't have a radio to call in the accident so decided we would report it when we got to Da Nang. We tried to catch up with the truck that killed the woman, but he was gone. We reported the incident to the first military policeman we saw. They weren't interested, so I reported it to my boss when we got back to Hill 37.

I drove that route for the next three days. Every day we would pass the dead woman. Nobody came to claim her body. On the third day, I brought an old blanket to cover her with if she were still there. She was. Her body was bloating in the sun and looking and smelling very bad. On the return trip from Da Nang that same day, we passed the dead woman's body again. Somebody had stolen the blanket from her body. On the fourth day, somebody finally removed the body. I felt bad for the old woman. I could not believe the driver of the truck didn't have the common decency to stop. The image of the woman lying there for three days still haunts me today.

I got back from my mail run one day and went to deliver the mail to Bock in the orderly room. He told me Kilo had just moved out to Hill 55. I wanted to go up to my old hootch and visit them before they left, but I was too late.

I noticed I had been getting fewer and fewer letters from my girlfriend. I really should have been getting more mail because school was out for the summer. I knew she had a summer job, but I still expected more mail. I did get a nice birthday card from her while I was in the hospital, so nothing led me to believe there was a problem.

One day, I got two unexpected letters from home. One was from a guy I went to high school with named Steve and the other from my girlfriend's mother. Steve was telling me that I had no right to keep my girlfriend from dating and I should do the right thing and break up with her. I didn't know why the hell he was writing me this stuff unless he wanted to date her. My girlfriend and I had an agreement that she could date. I wasn't stupid enough to believe she wouldn't; besides, I had enough friends back home that would write me and tell me what she was doing anyway. I didn't give it much more thought until I read her mother's letter.

Her mother started telling me how long distance relationships hardly ever worked out and when I returned home she "hoped" everything would work out for me. What? I had no idea what she was talking about so I wrote a letter to my girlfriend with my concerns. Up to that point, I was getting mail pretty regularly from my girlfriend, although I had been getting fewer letters than before, but I didn't have any cause for concern. About two weeks later, I got a reply from my girlfriend. She told me not to worry; everything was okay. She had gone out a couple of times with friends, but that was all. Most of the time, they went out in groups of four or five kids and just hung out. I wasn't worried. After all, I had been on R&R to Hong Kong, and I wasn't just buying suits.

As the month of July wore on, I was feeling much better. I got back from my mail run one day and the hill was a flurry of activity. I dumped the mail and went to headquarters to find out what was going on. The date was 28 July 1968. Bill and all the clerks were nervous. Bill told me Kilo Company had run into an "L" shaped ambush and was getting their asses kicked out in the Arizona Territory.

An "L" shaped ambush means they were hit on two sides, normally the front or rear and one flank. They had already reported a number of casualties and a battle was still raging in Dodge City. I knew Dodge City was a bad area, but it got worse as the day went on. I ran down to Bock to see if there was anything I could do. Everyone in Kilo Company who had been in the rear was gearing up to go out on a reaction force. I told Bock to tell them not to leave without me. I hauled ass back to my hootch and grabbed my battle gear. I loaded up with extra magazines and hand grenades. I took off back to headquarters to tell Bill I was going out on the reaction force with Kilo. Lt Boyer, my boss at the time, told me to stand fast. I would be needed at the LZ here.

Everyone in the rear area was forming up on the LZ when helicopters started coming in with wounded. The more seriously wounded were taken straight into Da Nang. I grabbed one of the wounded guys I knew and asked what had happened. He said Kilo was moving across a rice patty (or small lake) into Dodge City when all hell broke loose. It was a very well placed ambush by a very large, dug in NVA force estimated to be a company size unit numbering about 200 or more enemy soldiers. First Platoon got hit in the open and was taking massive casualties. Mike Company was on the way to help.

Helicopters continued to arrive with the wounded. I learned that Kilo had left Hill 55 the day before on 27 July on a company size search and destroy mission. They received incoming fire from a village they were about to enter and search. Two North Vietnamese soldiers were spotted running from the village after the firing ceased. The company entered, searched the village, and interrogated the inhabitants for any more enemy soldiers. Nothing was found, so the company commander decided to spend the night in the village. They were hit later that night with no casualties. A night ambush killed two NVA soldiers and they brought their bodies back into the village the next morning.

Later in the morning, the company commander decided to leave the village and sweep the area. After moving for about two hours, the two elements of the company were several hundred meters apart. Just about the time the unit was about to come back together, one of the platoons was ambushed. The platoon immediately reacted by charging the tree line from where the ambush had been initiated, just as they were taught. They walked into a meat grinder. Several Marines were killed instantly, and anyone who got up to help wounded Marines or move to a safer location was killed or wounded immediately. The large NVA unit had initiated a perfect L-shaped ambush and caught the entire platoon in the kill zone.

The other two platoons were ordered to move out to the decimated platoon's position to help. They were also ambushed and caught up in the fight. The NVA had snipers in well placed locations that were trained to take out the leaders. The company commander was wounded, as well as many of the junior leaders, radio operators, and corpsman. As calls for help started coming into the battalion, it was clear that one corporal was in charge of the company.

He immediately took control of the situation and reacted like a well seasoned Marine. Throughout the ambush, he moved from position to position caring for the wounded and encouraging the remaining Marines to continue the fight. He also began to call in supporting fire and medevac helicopters. He continued the assault on the tree line, attempting to break the back of the enemy and relieve the company from the devastating fire. The young Marine ran several times into that fire to drag wounded Marines to safety. He was credited with saving the lives of many Marines that day and breaking the back of the enemy with his ability to maintain control of the company.

He was submitted for the award of the Navy Cross, our Nation's second highest award for valor, for his actions that day. Unfortunately, the corporal never received his award. Apparently, his award recommendation was lost somewhere in the system. One of his platoon members, who was wounded that day, found out that he never received his award. That squad member is trying to revive the award action with the help of many of the Marines that were saved that day and also with the help of a Congressman from the state where he lives.

Many other Marines and Corpsmen reacted with valor that day also. Their efforts were well documented and appropriate awards were given. One such Corpsman was HM3 Wayne Caron. Wayne had only been in Kilo Company for twenty-five days when the ambush happened. Wayne was credited with saving the lives of three Marines while being wounded three times crawling to assist his wounded comrades. Wayne was finally killed by a rocket explosion. Wayne would receive the Congressional Medal of Honor for his actions that day. HM3 Caron's award citation can be read in Appendix B.

Four Silver Stars and a number of Bronze Stars with "V" device for valor were also awarded. More than two-thirds of the company would also receive Purple Hearts for their wounds. Kilo Company's losses included twenty-one killed in action, with seven more Marines dying later as a result of their wounds for a total of twenty-eight killed in action.

Around sixty Marines were wounded that day. Only thirty-three Marines, many of those wounded, were able to walk away from that ambush. The company was decimated, and was declared, "Combat ineffective."

The summary of casualties looked something like this:

28 Killed in action

60+ wounded and medevaced

33 not wounded and walking wounded

What was surprising to me was that the remaining thirty-three, many of them walking wounded, were ordered to walk back to Hill 55. I could not believe they had to walk out. Mike Company showed up to help with the gathering of all the equipment and finish gathering up the dead and wounded on the battlefield and help with the mop up operations. What remained of Kilo Company arrived on Hill 55 later that evening. The mood was somber. They were in a daze. I talked with several members of what was left of the company, and they just could not believe what had happened to them. To this day, at our reunions, that day is always on the minds of many, especially at our memorial service when the names of all Kilo Company's killed in action are read and the dates they were killed are read. So many on just one day.

Kilo Company was placed on stand-down. They did not have enough Marines left in the company to even make a platoon. I reported to my boss several days later and asked if I could return to Kilo Company. He sent me to the battalion aid station to see if the doctor would clear me to return. The battalion doctor told me I would have to be cleared by the doctors in Da Nang who had put the restriction on me from the beginning.

On another trip to Da Nang one day, I stopped by the NSA hospital to see if the doctor would release me from restricted duty. The doctor I had been seeing was gone. He had rotated back to the states. The new doctor told me he would have to find my file and look at it, then call me in for an examination. I told him I was feeling fine and just wanted to return to my company. He said he would be in touch with me. I never heard from the doctor again and remained on restricted duty for my remaining time in Vietnam. I was allowed to participate in several more operations with Kilo Company, but nothing to the extent as I had before getting sick. I continued convoy duties also and patrols into the village below our hill. I was placed in charge of many security details to take the doctors down to the village to help the civilians, but did not find it as rewarding as being with my squad.

Most of my friends from Kilo Company were either dead, wounded, or had rotated back to the states. Kilo Company seemed foreign to me. I still had a couple of friends there, but the longer I stayed in Headquarters Company, the more distant I felt.

A full list of the members of Kilo Company, Third Battalion, Seventh Marines and the dates they were killed in action can be found in Appendix C.

Pvt. Donald G. Tackett
Just out of the hospital before 28 July 1968 ambush

CHAPTER 16

BACK TO MY OLD SELF:
GETTING SHORT!

Do draft dodgers have reunions? If so, what do they talk about?

– UNKNOWN

I started feeling really good. I wasn't sick at all. I figured I'd try one more time to get back to Kilo Company. Since the ambush at the end of July, every available body was going to Kilo Company. I went to my boss who again told me to go to medical and get cleared. So I went to the battalion aid station and again tried to get him to clear me. I was once again told I could only be medically cleared by the doctor who put me on restricted duty to begin with. I decided not to fight it anymore. I had a good gig going now and figured I'd ride it out as long as I could.

Around the end of September, a bunch of us were sitting in the tent one evening cleaning our rifles before hole watch. I had met some real screw ups since I had been in Headquarters Company, but none matched this guy named Mark. Mark was from West Virginia and was not the smartest guy I'd ever met. He had been in the company for a couple of months now and was just goofy. You couldn't help but like him, though. Besides, he had a very good looking sister that was a senior in high school and a cheerleader. He showed us pictures of her, and we couldn't figure out for the life of us how in the hell that could be his sister! I asked him if I could start writing to her. I figured if things didn't work out with my girlfriend when I got home, I could go see her. I had a back-up plan.

Mark didn't like the fact I wanted to write to her, but gave me her address back home. He told me to go ahead, but she probably wouldn't be interested. A couple of weeks later, much to my surprise, I got a letter from her. For the rest of my time in country, we wrote to each other. We became very friendly, and I made plans to go visit Mark's family when I went home. I only had about three and a half months left now and started feeling like I was actually going to make it out of this place.

We were still receiving mortar and rocket attacks almost every night, so I kept my gear real close to me, not wanting to get killed with so little time left.

One night, we were cleaning our weapons when Mark started playing around with his. I told him to knock it off, but he continued to mess around. Bill and I were sitting on my bunk beside each other, and Mark was on another bunk next to ours facing us. Suddenly, Mark decided he was going to put a magazine in his weapon. We were only supposed to lock and load our weapons when we were on hole watch or leaving the perimeter. Then Mark did something that almost changed my life forever.

He pulled back the charging handle and put a round in the chamber of the weapon. As he let the bolt go forward, he had his finger on the trigger, and the rifle went off sending an M16 round whizzing by my ear between Bill and me. The round missed me by inches. I jumped up off the bunk and grabbed his weapon. I knocked him off his bunk and started beating the hell out of him. He had almost blown my head off! A few minutes later, the commander and first sergeant came running into the tent. Everyone was just watching me beat the hell out of Mark, but they grabbed me and separated the two of us. The commander was told what happened, and we both had to report to the orderly room.

I thought I was going to get busted by the commander for fighting, but after everyone explained to him what had happened, he let me go. A couple of days went by before Mark finally came up to me and apologized for his stupidity. I told him if I ever saw him do something like that again, I would shoot him myself. He knew I was serious.

At the end of September, the company had an awards and promotion ceremony. I hadn't been told I was going to receive anything, but had to attend anyway. About that time, the first sergeant called my name to come to the front of the formation where the company commander pinned the Purple Heart on my uniform that I had been awarded back in February when the truck I was in hit the mine. Then the first sergeant called several other Marines to the front also and told them to stand beside me. Mark was one of the ones called up.

Mark stood beside me. The first sergeant announced we were about to be promoted to corporal with the date of rank of 1 September 1968. What a surprise, an award and a promotion. The commander and first sergeant came up in front of each of us and pinned on our new stripes and handed us our promotion certificate. When the commander got in front of Mark, he held up his promotion certificate and tore it up right in front of the entire formation. That was his punishment for almost shooting me in the head. Mark would not be promoted during the rest of his time in Vietnam.

The first sergeant then dismissed the formation and asked me to come to his office. I didn't know what he wanted me for this time, but I was sure it couldn't be good. As I reported to him, he said he had heard I was an expert at burning crap on the shit burning detail.

I kind of laughed to myself and said, "Yes, I've spent a lot of time doing that."

He then told me I was the new non-commissioned officer in charge of the shit burning detail. I would get the detail started every morning and check on them until they were done. *Oh, my God, I thought I was done with that stuff.* He then told me that Mark would be on the detail every day until he left to go home. I could get my revenge on Mark for almost killing me.

I must have had a big grin on my face because the first sergeant said, "I knew you would like that."

Finally around the middle of October, I became a two digit midget. That means I had less than 100 days left in country. Ninety-nine days and a wake up. I was getting less and less mail from my girlfriend. I was thinking to myself that I should step up my writing campaign to Mark's sister, just in case.

I was eating chow with Bill one evening when he told me something that astonished me. He said he had extended his tour for six months because it was a sweet deal. The Marine Corps gave him thirty days free leave back to the states and flew him home for free. He said I should do the same. I thought about it, but decided that it would not be in my best interests. I had seen a lot of horrible things here, lost a lot of good friends, and decided to take my chances back in the states.

Bill then asked me if I would like to go on R&R to Bangkok, Thailand. I told him I already had an R&R, but he said it didn't matter because I was in a different company. I told him yes, and in a week I was on my way to Bangkok. The eight days I spent away from Hill 37 were fantastic. I had a great time in Thailand—from what I remember. I do know I drank a lot of liquor and threw up a lot. When I got back, Bill had left for his thirty days leave.

Sometime in November, I received my orders for my new unit when I returned to the states. I was being assigned to Camp Lejeune, North Carolina. I was excited. I was told I would probably be assigned to the rifle range to teach rifle marksmanship, since I was such a good shooter. I had another chance to qualify, and this time qualified expert.

As my time started to wind down, I started to get really slack in my job, my appearance, and my overall attitude. I was getting lazy again, and it was noticed by my boss. He didn't like it at all. I didn't really feel I had a bad attitude, but what did I know? I just wanted to go home. I hadn't heard from my girlfriend in about a month and was beginning to worry. I told myself she was involved in school and didn't have time to write so it wouldn't drive me crazy.

Around the first of December, we were told the entire battalion was going to move to Hill 10. I had about forty-five days left before heading home. Hill 10 was about half way between Hill 37 and Da Nang. That was good, not as far to travel to Da Nang for me. I was trying not to go into Da Nang so often now since I was getting short and about to go home. I had seen too many vehicles hit by roadside bombs while traveling that road. I was informed by the first sergeant that I would be in charge of convoy security during the move. It would take about three trips between hills to move all of Headquarters Company. I was not a happy camper. It was probably punishment for my lax behavior. We had plenty of extra Marines that could have done that job, but he picked me.

I decided to suck it up and drive on. The first two trips went off without incident. The last day of the move, I decided I would be on the last vehicle. I knew we would be eating a lot of dust, so I decided I would ride in the back of the truck. I climbed on top of a big tarp used to cover the equipment we were hauling so it wouldn't get all dusty. As we went down the road, I couldn't see a thing. I was covered with dust and dirt. I thought I would crawl under the tarp to get out of the dust, and I promptly fell asleep. I woke up just as we turned onto Hill 10. We reached the place to where we were to unload when I discovered my weapon was not on the truck. It must have fallen off the truck when I fell asleep. I started freaking out. It is a major sin to lose your weapon. I had done it again. I had screwed up bad this time. The offense for losing your weapon could land you in the brig, get you busted to private, or worse, dishonorably discharged. I was scared to death. In my own mind, I was back to the same idiot who had arrived a year ago a total screwup, and I would leave a total screw up.

I decided I had to report it to my boss. I went into my lieutenant's hootch and asked to speak to him. I could see the LT was not in a good mood, but I had to tell him what had happened anyway. I only had about forty days left in country at that time. I explained to the LT what had happened, and he just looked at me. He told me he couldn't believe how irresponsible I had been. He asked me if I had told anyone else. I said I hadn't. He then told me something that made me feel a little better. The LT told me I was a good Marine, and he would be glad to serve with me again in the future. However, I had to correct my mistake. He told me not to say anything to anybody, but I had better get my ass into Da Nang and find another weapon someplace, he didn't care from where and didn't want to know, but I had better have one within the next two days or he would be forced to report it to the company commander. I thanked him and left.

The next day I decided I had better make my move. I talked to two of my friends, explained what I had done, and asked if they were up for a little action. Of course, they were.

What I am about to tell you is something I have never told anyone. I was so ashamed of what I was about to do that I could not hold my head up very high and call myself a United States Marine.

My two friends and I drove to Da Nang that day and went straight to the 327 Hill PX. It was a huge area with shopping, a beer garden where you can drink beer and buy snacks, and an area for USO shows. If I was going to have to steal a weapon from a fellow service member, I refused to steal one from another Marine, so we had to look around. There were a bunch of drunks at the beer garden so that's where we went first. Everybody there was getting pretty rowdy, and we just didn't get a chance to snag one. Then, one of my friends came up and said he found a USO show going on around the corner and a company of Army grunts had grounded their gear by a big long building and only left two guards.

We went over to check it out and it looked promising. There was one guard on each end of the formation, and there were about a hundred sets of battle gear along with their weapons grounded there. They hadn't stacked their weapons like we were taught; they just laid the weapons across their packs, a very bad move. Stacking weapons makes them more secure because you have three or four in a stack locked together with the shoulder strap. If you stole one, you would have to steal all of them. We decided that my friends would go up and talk to the guards and distract them while I went through the building and out a side door to grab a weapon.

My friends split up and went around different sides of the building while I went inside. It was a big empty warehouse used to temporarily store gear. I was nervous as hell. Just stealing a weapon alone can be a court martial offense, but it was either that or me being court marshaled for losing mine. Anyway you looked at it, if I didn't do this, I was screwed. I noticed the guards were more interested in sitting in the shade and smoking and trying to see the USO show than watching their company's equipment. I saw my friends talking to them and glancing back in my direction. I took the chance, stepped out the open door and snatched an M16 off of a guy's gear. I walked casually back out the front door of the warehouse and back to where I told my friends we would meet. They showed up about five minutes later, and we left. I told my buddy to get us the hell out of there before the USO show ended and the guy I stole the weapon from found out his was gone.

I felt horrible for what I had done. I had committed a court martial offense. I thought to myself, *Maybe I should just turn myself in.* But got scared and decided to try not to show my face in Da Nang again until I was going home. MPs at every check point would be checking for that weapon. When we got back to Hill 10, I thanked my buddies for helping me and swore them to secrecy. I reported to my LT and told him the situation had been resolved. He didn't want to know how, just that I had a weapon.

When in a combat zone, it is not unusual to change weapons often. My first four months in country I had three different weapons. Even though we were issued a weapon by serial number, it is very unlikely we would turn in that very same weapon when we left. People know that, so when we turn in our weapon and the serial number doesn't match, it really doesn't matter. Weapons also get beaten up or damaged in combat, so I decided I would do my best to mess up the serial number. The serial number is on the magazine weld, so it wasn't too hard to mess it up. I scratched the serial number so several of the numbers could not be read and was satisfied it would not be discovered as stolen. I had never done something as low as that in my life and swore to myself I would never do anything like that again. I hoped the Army guys didn't get into much trouble, but with the way they were guarding their equipment, I'm surprised more stuff wasn't stolen. I knew there were slicky boys all over the place in Da Nang just waiting to steal from unsuspecting GI's, so I hoped that's exactly what the Infantry company I stole from thought.

From that time on I kept a very low profile in the area. I kept to myself, watched my attitude, and didn't bring any undue attention to myself.

There was talk going around that, if a Marine had been in country for one Christmas already, the Marine Corps was going to do their best to get them home before they had to spend two Christmas's in Vietnam. On 16 December, I had been in country for exactly a year. I only had thirty days to go. I didn't bother anyone about leaving to go home before Christmas because of what I had done a couple of weeks earlier. Like I said, I just wanted to keep a low profile. Christmas came again. I was on my second Christmas, but knew it was only a matter of days and I would be leaving. I only had twenty-one days and a wake up, and I would be going home.

On the morning of 26 December, I was in my hootch getting ready for shit burning detail when Sam came running into the tent. Sam said, "Don, I got you a flight date. You fly home in two days. Hurry, get packed, and catch the jeep leaving for Hill 55 in one hour." I was excited as hell. I was going to mail a bunch of stuff home because I couldn't carry it all but didn't have time now. I had war souvenirs I had collected while in the field with Kilo Company. I had the conical hat I had picked up when I shot at that VC when I first got there, an NVA pistol belt with a holster attached, a VC canteen, cover, and canteen cup, and a number of other smaller things. I had a pair of Ho Chi Minh sandals I found in a VC hiding area and a pair of black pajamas.

The guys in Headquarters Company were always jealous of my stuff. They had never been to the field and didn't have anything, so I was always on watch to make sure they wouldn't steal anything from me and kept my stuff locked in my footlocker.

I asked Sam if he would send me my war souvenirs, and he said, "Of course."

Well, guess what? I never saw any of my stuff again. Sam didn't send it to me, and I'm sure he's told many war stories of how he captured the enemy equipment himself when he got it home, along with any awards he might have awarded himself since he was a clerk. I guess it was pay back to me for the weapon I had stolen from the poor Army guy.

The last hurdle I had to jump was getting my gear turned into supply. Since I was turning it all into Headquarters Company supply, I figured there wouldn't be an issue with my mismatch serial number on my M16. Well, there was. The supply sergeant told me I would have to turn the weapon into Kilo supply since that's where I got it from. I only had an hour to get all my stuff together or I would not be able to go into Hill 55 or all the way into Da Nang until the next day, and I would probably miss my flight. We had to be there a day early to process out. I begged him to take it, but he was persistent. He did take all my other gear, even though it was filthy and I didn't have time to clean it because of my short notice to leave.

I ran down to Kilo supply, scared to death I was going to have a problem. The supply sergeant was there, and I talked to him, begging him to take the weapon even though I had not had a chance to clean it. He said, "No problem." He started looking at the serial number and said, "Damn, you must have seen a lot of action with this weapon. I can't even read the serial number." I asked if that was going to be a problem, and he said no. He got them in like that all the time. I had skated through. I also picked up my sea bag that had been stored in Kilo supply since I had gotten there. I thanked him and hauled ass back to my hootch to finish packing. Sam came in a few minutes later and had my orders in his hand. I opened my sea bag and everything in it was ruined. It was all damp and mildewed and still smelled like puke. The clothes inside were worthless. I threw everything in the corner and packed everything else up I could and headed for the jeep.

The driver put me in shock immediately. He told me we had to go back to Hill 37 and down Liberty Road to get to Hill 55. I was not a happy camper. I had seen too much action on that damn road and I didn't even have a weapon. There was another guy going, too. I was the senior man in the jeep so I rode in the front seat with the driver and told the other guy to sit in back and be prepared for anything. I told the driver to give me his M16 and to drive down Liberty Road like he had never driven it before. We headed out.

The trip to Hill 37 was no problem. When we got to the back gate of Hill 37 and started out, the gate guard stopped us. He said the mine sweep detail had been hit that morning, and we were heading out at our own risk. He would report to the duty officer that we were headed out

226

and wished us luck. I thought, *Good God! I hate this road!* That driver drove like he was driving the Indianapolis 500 race. I was impressed at his ability to avoid the holes and suspected places where mines could be buried. We arrived at Hill 55 unharmed. It seemed like he took the dog-leg left on two wheels we were moving so fast. I went into finance, drew my pay, and we had one more trip down the road to make, then on into Da Nang.

We arrived in Da Nang with no problem. The driver took me to the replacement station and dropped me off. I thanked him and wished him luck and walked off. I reported into the building that said "Outbound" and was scheduled for a flight the next day. We would fly into Okinawa, then on into El Toro Air Force Base, California.

Since I left Hill 10 in such a hurry, I decided I would find the barracks I would be staying in and repack my gear. I needed a good haircut as well as a good steam bath to get all the crud off of me. As I entered the barracks I was assigned, I saw two guys I knew from Kilo Company. One was a corporal I had attended ITR with and had flown over to Vietnam with. The other was a sergeant I knew. Both had survived the 28 July ambush. We talked a lot about what had happened and talked about the loss of our friends.

Another guy in the barracks told us the Bob Hope USO show was at the 327 Hill outside theater that day if we wanted to go. We all decided to go. The place was packed with GI's. We were so far away we could barely make out who was on stage. Bob Hope was very funny and then Ann Margaret came on stage. I wish I had my old set of binoculars about that time. We decided since we couldn't see, and could barely hear, we would leave. Jimmy had the same idea as me about going into Da Nang to get a haircut and a steam bath. The other guy wasn't that interested.

I noticed the sergeant had a beautiful war souvenir, a Russian SKS rifle with a folding bayonet. This was the war souvenir everyone wanted. I was jealous and told them about the stuff I had to leave behind, but that my buddy was going to send all of it to me. They just laughed. I guess they knew Bill wouldn't ever send it to me. The sergeant told me a lieutenant at the Replacement Center tried to take the SKS from him because the LT said he didn't have the correct documentation to take it home. They argued and the sergeant told the REMF LT he would have to pry it from his cold, dead, hands. About that time, a Marine gunnery sergeant came out of another office and broke up the confrontation. The gunny explained that the REMF's in the rear would try any trick to get the grunts to give up their war souvenirs. He gave the sergeant a letter authorizing him to carry it home, and the gunny said, "Good luck." Everyone was happy, except the LT.

Jimmy and I left the sergeant in the barracks to go find our steam bath and haircut, making sure the sergeant secured his SKS to his bunk with a chain and lock we found. Jimmy and I returned to the barracks later that night and had a few beers at the beer garden. We were both so excited we couldn't sleep that night and spent most of the night talking about getting home.

The next morning we were up, freshly shaved, washed, and had a clean set of camo fatigues and our boonie hats on. Hell, we even tried to shine our jungle boots, but only managed to get them black. The REMF's on our flight just stared at the three lean, mean, tanned grunts. All of us grunts seemed to hang together. You could definitely tell who had seen combat and who hadn't. Most of the people on our flight were wearing a khaki uniform with ribbons. All we had were our jungle camos and boonie hats. One senior officer asked us where our Khaki uniforms were. We told him they had been ruined while being kept in storage at our hill because we spent all our time in the bush. He seemed to accept our answer, and we weren't bothered about it again.

Finally, they started calling our names for the plane manifest. We waited. It took what seemed like forever before Jimmy's name was finally called. He boarded the plane and told me he would save me a seat. The sergeant was called next, and we said our good-byes. Finally, my name was called. I got on the plane and was fascinated at how cool the air on the plane felt. It was all of 100 degrees outside, and we were already sweating our butts off. I remembered when I had arrived over a year earlier looking at the guys headed home and being jealous of them. Now I was the one going home.

Everyone got settled in. An Air Force NCO came on board and took one more head count. I thought to myself, *Who the hell would miss this flight?* I was getting a little nervous because I remembered when we flew in and were told the VC liked to take shots at the plane and mortar the runway. We just wanted the damn plane to take off. When the doors shut, you could hear a pin drop. Then the pilot came on the intercom and said, "Ladies and Gentleman, welcome aboard Flying Tiger Airlines." A big cheer went up.

We were given last minute instructions and headed down the runway. We took our last look out the windows at the country that had caused us so much pain. The plane started down the runway and lifted off. When the wheels left the ground, another huge cheer came from everyone on board. I thought I was going to cry.

About thirty minutes later, the pilot came back on the intercom to say we had left Vietnamese airspace and were flying at cruising altitude.

I was a nineteen-year-old kid who had seen more death and destruction than one person should ever have to endure.

All I knew was I was going home.

Pvt. Donald G. Tackett

Donald and Bill

Pvt. Donald G. Tackett
Less than thirty days to go

CHAPTER 17
WELCOME HOME, DON

We would all like to live as we once lived, but history will not permit it.

– John F. Kennedy

This quote from JFK is very appropriate for this chapter in my life. I wanted my life to be exactly as it was before I entered the Marine Corps, but as everyone will see, that would not be the case.

At this point, I still hadn't told anyone I was coming home. I wasn't supposed to be home until the middle of January, more than two weeks away. I decided I would surprise everyone. It was a decision I would soon regret. After talking to Jimmy about it, he said he was going to call his parents so they could pick him up at the airport in Atlanta. He was from somewhere in Georgia. I stuck to my plan. Even though I wanted to call my mom and girlfriend, I did not. Surprise would be the order of the day. After the initial euphoria of leaving Vietnam, the feeling of being safe and knowing we would not have to return to that country finally hit us. Jimmy and I began feeling really nervous about the fact we were really heading home. We knew we had a layover in Okinawa, but didn't know how long we would be there. It really didn't matter to me because I knew I was safe.

We started wondering where and when we would get new uniforms. All of our stuff was ruined and all we had was what we were wearing. I had one fresh set of camo fatigues, but that was all. We figured we would get new stuff issued in Okinawa. I knew we would never be allowed to fly all the way home in our nasty looking jungle cammies. All I kept remembering was that Army MP at the Chicago airport when I had gone on leave from basic training. This time I knew I would not put up with any of his crap. I was a salty, seasoned, combat Marine, and not one to be messed with.

We had both sort of nodded off for a little while when the pilot came on the intercom to say we were about to land in Okinawa. He thanked us for our service and said it was his honor to be our pilot. I thought that was very nice of him. Little did I know, but it would be the last "thank you" I would receive for a very long time.

The landing was just a simple landing, nothing like landing in Vietnam, when it felt like the plane was about to crash because the pilot landed so fast and steep. Once the plane came to a complete stop an Air Force NCO came on board to give us our directions. I sure would like to know how someone gets a gig like those Air Force guys had. The officers were sent in one direction, and all of us Marines were sent to a different bus from everyone else. I never could figure out why the Marines were separated from everyone else, but we were. We were bussed out to a place called Camp Hansen. When we arrived, a young looking Marine staff sergeant came on the bus to brief us. He had us follow him into a building where we were issued sheets, pillow cases, and one blanket. We were then led to a barracks building with real mattresses, hot showers, and a real head with doors on the stalls for privacy. For over a year, I was used to going to the head to take care of business and hold a conversation with the guy sitting on my left or right. The staff sergeant told us to stow our gear and meet him back in front of the barracks, and he would explain what the next couple of days would bring.

Jimmy and I found our bunks, stowed our gear, and went outside with the rest of the Marines. There were about thirty of us out there all wondering when we would fly on home. The same young Marine came out of the orderly room with a clip board and started calling out the names of the Marines that would fly out the very next day. About five or ten names were called, but Jimmy and I were not that lucky. He said all the Marines that did not have uniforms would meet up with him the next day, and he would take us to have one khaki uniform issued. We would have to buy our ribbons, but they would issue everything else. We could have our stripes sewn on right there before we left and then give them to the tailor who would have them cleaned, pressed, and returned to us the same afternoon. They had the process down pretty well. I was impressed with the efficiency of their operation. I guess they had done it so much by now that it was just another day at work; a far cry from what Jimmy and I had just came from.

On the bus ride back, we asked the Marine when we could expect to leave. More Marines were arriving to Camp Hansen returning from Vietnam, and we didn't want to get caught up in the mess. The Marine said they had a list of flights and had so many seats allocated for just Marines. Sometimes he would get five seats; sometimes he would get twenty seats; it just depended on the other services and how many seats they had been given. We would depart in the same order as we arrived. As for when our names would be called, there were normally two to three flights a day, so we had to be ready to go at any time. No problem there.

Jimmy and I got our stuff together and waited. The next morning he called us all out and began calling names. Again, Jimmy and I were not called. Around 1300 hours, another formation. Again, our names were not called. It was now 27 December 1968. Finally, that evening around 1700 hours, the Marine called us out again. This time Jimmy and I had our names called. We had a flight at midnight. Very cool. We were very excited.

Around 2100 hours, about six of us loaded a bus going to the airport. We got to the airport and checked in. The Marine wished us luck and departed. We checked in with an Air Force NCO at a counter that looked just like a check in place at any civilian airport. He put us on the manifest and told us the plane would load up around 2300 hours. Finally, the time came for us to load up. We lined up and got on the plane and got settled in. This time there were a lot of civilians on the flight. That didn't bother me, but it was cool seeing civilians again.

The same Air Force NCO came on the plane with a clip board. He got on the intercom and said, "The following individual's need to depart the plane immediately." Three names were called and then Jimmy and I were called and told to depart the plane. We couldn't figure out why, but we did as ordered. We went back into the terminal as five civilians passed us getting on the plane and taking our seats. We asked the Air Force guy what was happening, but he only said he would explain in a minute. The plane's door closed, and it was gone. We were stunned. The Air Force guy came back in and said the plane had been overbooked and since we were not paying customers, we had to leave the plane. I thought, *Hell. We just paid for our tickets fighting a war!* He said there was another plane scheduled in the morning, and he would make sure we were on it.

We were pissed off and had no choice but to stand by and wait until morning. About 0600 hours the next morning, the terminal started to become a flurry of activity. Both civilians and military people started showing up in huge numbers. A plane landed and unloaded its cargo of people. Another Air Force NCO showed up at the counter so we went up to talk to him. We told him what had happened the night before and that we were supposed to be on the flight that just landed. He checked his manifest and said we were not on it. He said the best he could do was get us transportation back to Camp Hansen. As promised, a vehicle showed up and took us back.

The Marine NCO inside the orderly room was surprised to see us. He said he would take care of it and get back with us. It was now 28 December 1968. Finally the next day, he called our names again. We went through the same routine. We got on the plane that afternoon only to have an Air Force NCO pull us off again and load civilians in our place. This was beginning to get crazy. We were taken back to Camp Hansen one more time. Again, the Marine was surprised to see us. We were fit to be tied. We asked him what was going on. He could only explain that civilians stationed on Okinawa had purchased tickets to go back to the states on vacation for the New Year and they had priority. We couldn't believe what we were hearing.

Again on the twenty-ninth, our names were called. We would be flying out around 1500 hours. We, again, went through the same routine returning to the airport terminal. This time our names were called and we got on the plane. Jimmy and I fastened our seat belts and said to each other that they would have to drag our asses off this plane if our names were called this time. I guess we must have been talking too loud because an Army colonel was sitting across the aisle from us, listening and giving us a dirty look. He asked me what the problem was. I almost lost it, but held my composure long enough to explain to him what had been happening for the last three days.

About that time, the Air Force NCO came on the plane with his clipboard. He grabbed the intercom while flipping through his papers. We saw the colonel get up out of his seat and make his way to the front of the aircraft. The colonel took the NCO outside the aircraft door. A few minutes later, the colonel re-entered the aircraft, but the Air Force NCO did not. The door closed and we were going to leave Okinawa. The colonel sat back down and grinned at us. All we could do was thank him for his help. He told us not to worry about it and if we would permit it, he would like to buy us a beer once the plane was in the air. He saw our ribbons, saw our Purple Hearts and asked us how we had gotten wounded.

Jimmy and I explained our stories and the colonel said, "Hell, I'll buy you two beers!"

Once the plane reached cruising altitude and the flight attendants came around, the colonel kept his promise. He bought us each two beers. Those were the best tasting beers we had ever had. We tried to buy the colonel a beer back, but he wouldn't hear of it. We had made an Army friend. I wish I could remember the colonel's name. We toasted each other with our cold beers and enjoyed the colonel's company. The colonel told us he had been an infantry company commander during the Korean War. We hadn't really noticed it before because we were so pissed off, but the colonel was very highly decorated with a Silver Star, two Bronze Stars with "V" device, and three Purple Hearts. He was also wearing the Army's Combat Infantryman's Badge. We were proud to be acquainted with such a war hero. We knew he had been through the shit just like we had, probably worse. All we knew was that war is hell.

Jimmy and I settled in for the long flight to California. There would not be a stop in Hawaii on the way back. After we drank our beers with the colonel and finished all the talking, it was time to try to rest. Our feet were killing us because we had not worn low quarters (shoes) in more than a year. Even when we went on R&R, we wore tennis shoes or boots. We decided to give our feet a break and take off our shoes and relax. The way it smelled in the plane we figured a bunch of others decided to do the same. That smell was nothing like the smells in Vietnam, so it didn't bother us at all.

After what seemed like forever, the pilot came on the intercom and announced we were beginning our descent into the United States. We would be landing at El Toro Air Force Base, California. He said there would be plenty of transportation available to take us on to LAX. We were getting really excited again. As we tried to put our shoes back on, we discovered our feet had swollen so badly, we could not get them back into our shoes. We tried standing up and walking to get the swelling to go down, but our feet just weren't going back into those shoes. We decided to carry our shoes off the plane and try again in the terminal.

The plane touched down and a big yell came up from all the GI's on board. The civilians looked more disgusted with us than happy we were home, but we didn't care. We looked over at the colonel and thanked him for his kindness and he wished us well. Once again the familiar Air Force NCO came on board the plane and told all of the GI's on the plane to stay seated while the officers and civilians departed the plane first. We were beginning to feel more and more like second class citizens as opposed to returning warriors.

We were the last to unload. We were all herded into a side building away from the terminal and told we had to have a briefing before departing on leave. Our leave forms would be stamped there and our leave time would begin then instead of when we flew out of Vietnam. Jimmy and I carried our shoes off the plane and received glares and stares, but nobody said anything. We went into a big room where several tables were set up, had our leave forms stamped, and then were led to another waiting area. When everyone was finished with their leave forms, an officer came in to brief us.

The officer told us we would not be allowed to wear our uniforms to LAX. He said that because of all the war protesters and problems previous GI's were having at the airport, they thought it was better for us to be in civilian clothes. All I had were the clothes I had worn on R&R that hadn't been ruined. We were all in shock. I could not believe we couldn't wear our uniforms. I was proud to be a United States Marine and didn't care who knew it.

We went ahead and changed clothes, grumbling about it the entire time. We were thinking, "Hell, with these haircuts and carrying sea bags, don't they think the protesters would know we were in the service?" It sounded ridiculous to us that we had to change. All I had were short sleeve shirts and khaki pants, no coat yet. I was headed for Ohio in the middle of winter. I thought I might be able to buy a jacket at the airport.

About five of us guys met outside and hired a taxi to take us to the airport. The taxi driver jammed all our bags in the trunk, we squeezed into the taxi, and off we went. We arrived awhile later at the airport. It seemed like a different world. There were people everywhere. We did see war protesters and some Hare Krishnas running around in sheets singing, but we were on a mission to get home. We went inside not knowing where to go or what to do.

One of the guys with us said, "Lets all go to the first counter with the shortest line and go." We did.

The only flight I could get had two stops before we arrived in Columbus, Ohio. The first stop was in Phoenix. I had about an eighteen hour layover. I remembered my brother was stationed there, so I figured he could pick me up and I could go to his house until my flight early the next morning. The next stop was in Chicago. I hated that airport, but if it was one more step to getting home, then so be it. I got my tickets and said my good-byes to Jimmy. He got a flight straight to Atlanta and was leaving very soon. I would not see Jimmy again until the Kilo Third of the Seventh reunion in Louisville, Kentucky, in 2002.

I had about an hour before my plane left, so I called information in Phoenix and got my brother's phone number. He was home and happy to hear from me. I hadn't talked to him for almost two years. He would pick me up at the airport. I told him not to call home and tell mom because I wanted to surprise her. He said okay. The plane ride was a short one. Nothing like the flight from Okinawa to California.

I started noticing people staring at me. At first, I thought it might have been my imagination, but after a while I figured it was because of my close cut, high-and-tight haircut and the green little bag I was carrying with a Marine Corps emblem on it. It was like they knew where I had just come from. I was tanned, clean cut and good looking (as far as I was concerned anyway).

My brother and his wife picked me up at the airport. After a short reunion, we went to the counter to confirm my flight on into Chicago and eventually Columbus. I didn't buy a jacket in the airport in California, so my brother offered to lend me one. I declined. A bad decision. I really wasn't thinking about the weather in Ohio. We went to my brother's house and had a good visit. My next flight wasn't for another fourteen hours or so. My sister-in-law was making dinner when my brother asked me if I wanted to go out into the desert outside his home and shoot his .22 caliber rifle at rats.

I said, "Why not?"

It was not until many years later, when my brother and I were talking, that he told me how strange I was acting that day out in the desert. He said I seemed nervous and on edge. He said I kept pointing out areas in the terrain that would make great gook ambush sites. I was apparently walking like I was on point in the jungle looking for ambushes and booby traps. I didn't notice my strange behavior at the time.

Finally, the time came for my next leg of the trip. My flight to Chicago left Phoenix early the next morning, 31 December 1968. I thought it would be a great time to surprise my family and girlfriend: New Years Eve. I figured I would spend some time with my family, then drive to my girlfriend's house and surprise her. She would be out of school for Christmas break. I knew she would know where some New Year's Eve parties would be, and we would go and surprise all my friends, too. The only thing that worried me was the weather. My plane was due to land in Columbus around 1300 hours that day. If the weather held, there would be no delays, and I could get a taxi to the bus station and take a bus the last fifty miles to my home in Zanesville. My mom should still be at her work, and I could walk from the bus station to her work and ride home with her. Perfect plan. Now if I could only execute it.

So far, so good. There were no delays in Chicago, and my flight to Columbus went off without a hitch. I arrived in Columbus to a very bad storm brewing. Snow was beginning to fall, it was cold as hell, and the roads were about to freeze. It was only one o'clock in the afternoon, but it looked like early evening because it was so cloudy. If the highway froze from Columbus to Zanesville, I would be stuck and my plans would go to hell in a hand basket. I walked outside in my short sleeve shirt, hauling my sea bag and ditty bag, looking for a taxi. I found one and asked him how much he would charge me to drive me all the way into Zanesville. I don't remember how much the taxi driver told me, but it was way more money than I had. He took me to the bus station and wished me luck.

I ran into the bus station, and it was nearly empty. It was New Years Eve, bad weather was coming in. Only a fool like me would be out in that weather on that day. I went up to the counter and the lady behind it looked over her glasses as if to say, "Where the hell did you come from?" I told her that I had just come home from Vietnam and was trying to get to Zanesville.

She said, "A bus is due in from Indianapolis anytime now, if the weather didn't stop it."

It was going through Zanesville and on to Pittsburg. The time was now 1430 hours. I was cutting this too damn close. I waited for what seemed like forever, but it was actually only about thirty minutes until the bus arrived. He unloaded his cargo, and I got on. He said I was his only stop in Zanesville, and we had better get moving. He wanted to make it to Pittsburg, and the weather was moving in on him fast.

I sat on the bus and watched the weather get worse. The bus only had to travel fifty miles, but it seemed like it was taking forever. We finally arrived in Zanesville about an hour later. It was about 1600 hours on a Tuesday, and my mom worked at a jewelry store about three blocks from the bus station. I knew they would be open because I remember in years past her working until they closed at five o'clock, even on New Year's Eve. I hoped Mr. Engle, the owner, didn't close the store early because of the weather. Then laughed to myself, knowing how cheap he was. He was not about to close the store because of weather. He never had before. If he had closed it, I would freeze to death waiting for someone to come and get me.

It was a very long, cold, wet, snowy walk to the store. I was still in my short sleeve shirt. I stood in front of the store for a minute, and yes, it was still open. I could see my mom at her usual place in the back of the store where she was the cashier. I quietly walked in. Mr. Engle was the first to see me. I held my finger to my mouth as if to shush him. I wanted to surprise Mom. He got it, took my sea bag from, me and had me walk behind him to the rear of the store where my mother was.

Mr. Engle was a big man so it wasn't hard to hide behind him. Mom looked up wondering what was going because Mr. Engle had a huge smile on his face. Then I stepped out from behind him. Mom's mouth flew open and she was definitely surprised. She ran from behind the counter, crying and smiling at the same time.

The first thing she said to me was, "Silly boy, where is your coat?" We hugged for a few minutes and then she finally let me go.

She said, "Why didn't you call so we could pick you up?" I just said I wanted to surprise everyone. Mission Accomplished.

Mr. Engle knew mom wasn't going to be able to finish her work, so he told her to go on home. He offered me one of his coats, but I said no. We had to walk another two blocks to where my mom parked her car. I wanted to drive because I hadn't driven in over a year. We drove home with her talking a mile a minute. I couldn't get a word in. When we got home, I told mom I wanted to go to my girlfriend's house at 1900 hours. She said, "What the hell is 1900 hours?" I corrected myself and said, "Seven o'clock." She said okay; she understood. We would have plenty of time to catch up later.

My aunt, who still lived with us, almost had a heart attack when I walked in the back door. She hugged me and cried for about ten minutes. My mom got on the phone and called my oldest brother, who only lived around the corner, and told him I was home. He and his wife and two kids came right over. Of course, my aunt wanted to feed me. That's what she always did. She had taken care of us since my dad died in 1963. My mom had gone back to school and worked full time, so my aunt lived with us to help out. She could really cook. I told her I wasn't hungry but did want to get a quick bath, get some fresh clothes on, and go to my girlfriends.

This entire time my idiot stepfather stood back, as if I had just invaded his territory. He was indifferent to the whole situation. He made a vain attempt to welcome me home, but it was empty and shallow. He said I should have called, and he would have picked me up. But he would have been the last one I would have called. He would have probably wanted gas money.

I had been wearing the same clothes for two days now and really wanted to get cleaned up and get into something warm. I took a quick bath, something I had not done in more than a year, and got my old clothes out of the closet. I had lost weight over there, but everything still fit pretty well. I put on a jacket and didn't take it off the rest of the night, still trying to thaw out. As I looked in the mirror, I couldn't believe how good I looked. I had definitely changed. I was a lean, mean, fighting machine. I smiled.

Finally around seven o'clock, I excused myself, went upstairs and splashed on some more Brut Cologne, borrowed my mom's car, and headed for the destination I had been waiting for the most. I could not wait to see my girlfriend again. I had only gotten a couple of letters from her in my last month or so in country, but kept telling myself she was busy in school. The weather was slacking off. It stopped snowing, and it seemed like the moon was out. It was a beautiful New Year's Eve. It only took about fifteen to twenty minutes to drive to the other side of town where she lived. I pulled up in front of her house with much anticipation of what the evening would bring. I noticed the car that her father had bought her for graduation was still in the driveway along with her father's car, so I knew they were home. I figured her mother and father would be out for the evening, but they weren't.

I never went to the front door when I went to her house. I always went to the side door along the driveway. That door led onto a small landing. If I turned right on the landing, I could go down to the basement or go straight up two steps and be in the kitchen. I was as nervous as I had ever been in my life. I knocked on the side door, hoping she would answer. A few knocks later, and the outside light came on and the door opened. It was her mom. She put her hands to her face and started crying. She grabbed me and took me inside, hugging me the whole time. We went into the kitchen with her still hugging me. She yelled for her husband to come and see who was there. My girlfriend's dad came in and had a huge smile on his face. He grabbed my hand and started shaking it as if I were a long lost relative. I knew they always liked me, but I didn't know they liked me that much. We talked for a couple of minutes, with me expecting an appearance from my girlfriend. She must have heard all the commotion by now. Her younger brother was there and welcomed me home too.

I asked if my girlfriend was home, and her mom said, "Yes of course, she's upstairs getting ready to go out."

Perfect. Everything was working out perfectly. I figured she was probably going out with friends, so she and I would drive and join them.

Her mom and dad led me into the living room. Her mom went up stairs to get my girl while her dad sat down on his recliner. Her brother excused himself and left to go out with some friends that had just showed up to pick him up. Her dad and I made small talk, and he even offered me a beer. That was something I never thought he would do. I politely declined, even though I really could have used one. My mouth was dry, and my anticipation and impatience were growing by the second.

Her mom came back downstairs and took her seat in her recliner. I was sitting on the end of their couch. Her mom said my girl would be down in a minute. Time seemed to drag by. I figured she was getting herself all dolled up for me and that's what was taking so long. Finally, I heard her bedroom door close and heard her coming down the stairs. I stood up and waited for the biggest hug of any of the hugs I had gotten to this point.

To my surprise, she still had on a house coat. She reached the bottom of the stairs with a strange little smile on her face. I will never forget the look in her eyes. It was almost a fearful look. Instead of running into my arms, she said hello and sat down on the other end of the couch. I didn't think she was embarrassed to hug and kiss me because she had done it before in front of her mom and dad. I chalked it up to her being nervous and in shock because I had surprised her.

We made small talk for a little while and I could see her mom wiping tears from her eyes. I didn't know what the hell was going on. Her father excused himself and went into the kitchen.

I finally said to my girlfriend, You probably know where there's a party going on. Why don't you get dressed and we can go out?"

She then got this really strange look on her face, looked down, and said, and I will never forget this as long as I live, "I can't. I've got a date."

I couldn't breathe. A huge lump came up in my throat. I was in shock. I could not believe what I had just heard. Her mother started crying and left the room to go upstairs. She said something like, "I can't believe you" to her daughter.

We were alone in the living room now, and I was still trying to figure out what had just happened. I started to think, *Is this some kind of joke?* But it wasn't. She was serious. My heart was broken. I asked her what was going on. She said she wished I would have called her before I got home, and she wouldn't have made plans.

I said, "Forget your plans, I'm home! I'm sure whoever it is will understand."

She said no, she wasn't going to break her plans. She told me to call her the next day, and we could go out and talk. I was probably tearing up myself by then and was in complete shock. I got up and walked to the kitchen to go out the side door. Her dad walked by me saying he was sorry and patted me on the shoulder. My girlfriend was close behind me.

I got to the landing of the stairs and turned around. She was at the top of the stairs not two feet from me. I just wanted to grab her and kiss her to try to remind her of how close we once were. I just stood there looking at her. She said she was sorry several times, but by now, sorry just wasn't good enough. I asked her why she just didn't write me and tell me she didn't want to see me anymore or, that she had found someone else. She said she still wanted to see me, but just not tonight. She again asked me to call her the next day. I asked again why she just didn't write me and tell me. She said something that brought back memories of my friend Steve Davis and the possibility that he got a Dear John letter and that may have been why he died.

She said, "I didn't want you to go off and do something stupid." Again, all I could think of was Steve.

I stood there a few more minutes, not knowing what to say or how to convince her to change her mind. She was crying now, and I guess that's why I didn't say anything nasty to her. I was thinking of some things I wanted to say, but just couldn't do it. It was New Years Eve, 1968, and I was alone—again. Welcome home, Don.

CHAPTER 18

REVENGE

He that has revenge in his power and does not use it, is the greater man.

— Wellins Calcott

I sat in my car in front of my girlfriend's house, in the freezing cold, trying to absorb what had just happened to me. I was dazed and confused. The longer I sat there, the more pissed off I got. My only thought was revenge. I figured I would sit there until the unfortunate individual who was about to pick up my girlfriend showed up. My thought was, I would get out, beat the crap out of him, and leave him in a bloody mess in her front yard. Then I got this bright idea. Instead of kicking his ass there, I would go down the street to the 7-Eleven and get me some beer, park on the corner. When he showed up and they left for their party, I would follow them and confront them at the party. I could probably even pick me up a girl there and possibly make her jealous.

I drove around the corner, where I knew a 7-Eleven was. I hoped the guy wouldn't ask for my ID card because I was still only nineteen years old. I thought I really needed that beer for courage. The old 7-Eleven was closed, so I had to drive a couple of miles down the road before I found one still open. I went in, grabbed two quarts of beer, and bought them without any questions asked. I drove back to her house and parked on the street corner by a tree so my car would be partially blocked from view. I had a solid plan, or so I thought.

I drank the first quart of beer rather fast, too fast. It gave me the familiar buzz I would usually get that told me to stop drinking. I must have waited for at least an hour when I decided that he must have showed up when I was out getting beer. I finished the second quart and planned my next move. I went back to the 7-Eleven and used the pay phone to call one of my old friends. He was married then, so I figured he would still be at home. He answered and was surprised to hear it was me. I told him what had happened and that I wanted him to go with me to find her. Our town was a small one, so I knew where they probably would be. He told me where he and his wife lived and told me to come on over, and we would figure something out.

I arrived a little while later. I was glad they didn't live far from my girlfriend because I obviously should not have been driving. I went in and he and his wife welcomed me home.

He said, "Look, we are not going to be able to find them tonight, but a bunch of our friends are coming over to celebrate New Year's Eve with us and you can stay here for the rest of the night."

I told him I would hang around for a little while to see everyone, but I was going to leave to find my girlfriend and her date. I was determined I was going to ruin my girlfriend's evening, just like she had ruined mine. As people started showing up, the beer started flowing. I temporarily forgot all about what had happened earlier and began to enjoy myself. Somewhere around eleven o'clock, I decided I was going to leave. I was drunk as a skunk, and that was not such a good idea. Little did I know, my buddy's wife had taken my keys and hidden them. I looked all over the place as they continued to ply me with beer, hoping I would pass out soon. I do remember midnight, but barely. I promptly passed out. I woke up the next morning on my buddy's couch with one hell of a hangover.

My buddy and his wife were awake and fixing breakfast. All I wanted was some coffee and aspirin. We talked about the previous evening and how they talked me out of trying to find my girlfriend and her date. I kind of figured who it was, but I really didn't know for sure. I found out later it was the guy that wrote me the letter the previous July telling me to break up with her. I was glad they didn't let me drive that night because I would have ended up in jail, either from assault or DUI.

I went on home and everyone was up and moving about. My mom looked at me when I came in the door and said, "What in the world happened to you?"

I told her what happened and she said she was sorry. She asked me if I was going to call my girlfriend—by then I guess she was my ex-girlfriend—and I said no. My pride was hurt and my ego shattered. All I wanted to do was forget about her.

I ran into my ex-girlfriend's dad a couple of days later when I was downtown eating lunch. I was supposed to meet my mom for lunch that day, but something came up and she couldn't make it. I was sitting in a corner booth when he came up and asked if he could join me. I said, of course. I was glad to see him. I liked him and he had always liked me. We started talking and he asked me some questions about Vietnam, but I could tell there was something else on his mind. He then said he was sorry for what his daughter had done to me New Years Eve. He also asked me if I was going to call her. I told him I didn't know if I would or not. He said he wouldn't blame me if I didn't. I told him I didn't have any hard feelings towards her, but I was still trying to figure out what I was going to do. He said he hoped I called her. Figures, she left me for a freaking hippie. He said he overheard her talking to her mother one morning, and she was asking her mother if she thought I would call. Her mother suggested to her that she call me. She should apologize.

I finally made the rounds visiting friends and relatives and decided it was time to get on with my life. I decided it was best I didn't call her. I was hurt and didn't want to have to go through that again. I still had a year and a half left in the Marine Corps, and I couldn't stand to come home to another homecoming like I just experienced. I had to let it go. There was a very real possibility I would go back to Vietnam.

One of my single friends, Ken, said we should go out to this local bar where all the college kids hung out called, Swallows that Friday night. I know, the name sounds funny, but before your mind goes in the gutter, it was named for the birds that seemed to be everywhere around there. It was my first Friday night at home. I got all cleaned up with my nice pants, shirt, jacket, high-and-tight haircut, and, of course, my Brut Cologne. I still have the empty bottle to this day. As we pulled up in the parking lot, we could see it was the place to be. We could barely find a place to park. It was my first Friday night home, and I hoped to run into some of the girls I went to high school with or maybe even my ex-girlfriend. I was ready to find some female companionship.

We walked in and the place was crowded. It was smoky and kind of smelled. We looked around and found two seats at the bar. It was a perfect location to scout out the girls. I remembered seeing at least ten guys and girls I had known over the years. Nobody seemed to pay a bit of attention to me. I was surprised because many of them I had grown up with and had been good friends with. The one thing they all had in common was they were all hippies or at least they dressed like hippies. I was the only one in the entire place that was dressed nice and looked presentable. My buddy Ken wasn't a hippie, but he did have rather long hair for my taste.

All of a sudden, someone came up behind me and put their hands over my eyes. It surprised me and I almost turned around and decked them, but I figured out real quick it was a girl because of the big breasts pressed against my back.

She said, "Guess who?" I let her stand there for a little bit while I made several attempts to try to figure out who it was. I was in no hurry. It just felt good to have a girl that close to me again.

I finally grabbed her hands off my eyes and turned around. It was a girl I had known for years. Her name was Margo. She went to the Catholic school with my friend Pat. I had met her years ago when we used to go to the Catholic Youth Activity dances. Oh my, had she changed. She had always liked me, but I wasn't that into her. She was a nice girl, but not really my type. We hugged each

255

other, and it felt good to finally talk to a girl. She had also blossomed. She was looking good. She had long blond hair and was dressed in a mini skirt. She smelled good, too. Hell, everybody dressed like a hippy back then, but the girls looked good in miniskirts. Ken wondered off, and I sat and enjoyed the company of Margo for the rest of the evening. Again, what surprised me the most about that evening was that I could see at least ten people I grew up with in the bar and not one of them came up and said hello.

Margo didn't have a clue I had joined the Marine Corps or that I had just returned from Vietnam, so we had a conversation about that. She also knew I had a girlfriend, so she asked me where she was. I went through the entire story of my surprise homecoming. It felt strange to talk about my ex-girlfriend, and I started having feelings for her again. I was thinking to myself, *I should call her tomorrow.* Margo said she would see her in the bar on occasion with people, but didn't know she had been dating anyone else. She was holding on to me the entire evening. We talked and talked. I was beginning to feel normal again. Finally, around midnight Ken was ready to go. He was pretty drunk so I thought I had better take him home. Margo hugged and kissed me and gave me her phone number. The bar didn't close until two-thirty in the morning, so I told her I would take Ken home and be right back. When I returned about an hour later, Margo had left.

I dated her several more times before my leave was up. I was left sitting at the bar talking to the bartender the rest of the night with several guys trying to give me the stare down. I was feeling a little paranoid. The bartender said they had been talking about me when I left. They said they knew me but didn't know where I had been since we graduated a year and a half before, but figured I was in the military. I told the bartender I was in the Marine Corps and had just returned from Vietnam. The bartender would not let me pay for any more beer that night. I had a good time and repeated the night several more times while I was on leave. I didn't call my ex-girlfriend the next day.

Paranoia kept creeping up on me. I was always feeling like people were staring at me. I had never had that feeling before I joined the Marines, and I didn't like it. It would later cause me to get into many fights that I would never have gotten into.

The second week I was home, I was driving downtown to pick up my mom for lunch. I had been driving her car since I got home and didn't want her to have to catch a ride with her friend. Besides, I liked spending time with her away from my idiot stepfather. As I got off the exit leading to downtown, I saw my ex-girlfriend getting out of a blue Volkswagen bug at the local library. Not to my surprise, the guy getting out of the driver's side was the guy who wrote me the letter in July. I just confirmed what I already knew. I honked my horn, smiled and waved at her. She gave me a sheepish little smile and waved back. He just stared. It wouldn't be long before I saw that Volkswagen again. I had lunch with my mom and then shopped around town and just kind of hung out.

I got home about three hours later. My aunt told me I had a phone call from my ex-girlfriend. She wanted me to call her when I got a chance. I had very mixed emotions about calling her. I really did want to talk to her, but I was nervous. I was not prepared for any reasons or excuses she might have for doing what she did to me. I did not return her call. I saw her several times while I was on leave in passing, but only smiled and waved. Maybe I should have called to get my feelings off my chest, but I figured it just wasn't worth it. I was not out to hurt her. She could go on with her life, and I could go on with mine.

Towards the end of my second week home, I was sitting one afternoon at one of those drive-in type restaurants where they come out and put your tray on the window. I was parked facing Maple Avenue, the main drag where all the kids would cruise in their cars. I was hoping to run into some more of my old friends. I was eating and minding my own business when I noticed the familiar blue Volkswagen bug coming from my left. It was him. He noticed me sitting there. My mom's car was a very nice Pontiac Lemans, bright red with a black convertible top. It was very noticeable. He stared at me as he drove on. I didn't pay him much attention and continued to eat. A few minutes later while watching the traffic, I saw the blue Volkswagen bug coming back down the street to my right. This time as he drove by, he stuck his hand out the window and gave me the finger the entire time staring at me. I freaked the hell out.

I threw the tray off my window and hauled ass out of the parking lot after him. Because of the traffic, by the time I was able to pull out on Maple Avenue, he was gone. I knew where he lived in our small town, so I went to his house. He was walking out of his garage when he saw me pull up. He had his books in his hands and just stopped and stared at me. This was the part that became very fuzzy for me. I got out of the car and just remembered running up through his yard and knocking the hell out of him. He dropped his books and made a vain attempt to fight back and protect himself. I was on him like a wild animal. I had him on the ground and was just whaling on him. About that time, his father and mother came out the door. His father grabbed me, so I turned on him. I was about to knock the crap out of his dad when I heard his mom say she was calling the police. His son was still on the ground holding his face. I must have had a look to kill in my eyes because his father held both his hands up and told me to get the hell off his property.

I walked back down the yard, got into my car, and went home. When I walked into the house, my mom asked what was wrong. I told her and then said that the police would probably be showing up soon. It didn't take long. I was sitting in the living room in the exact same spot I sat in when the Marine Corps recruiter came to my house in what seemed like a long time ago. Fortunately for me, I knew the police officer. He was the father of a kid I had gone to school with for years. He knew my family and me very well.

He knocked on the door and my mother let him in. He came into the living room and I stood up. He said his son had told him I had joined the Marine Corps and said it was good to see me again; too bad it was under those circumstances. He told me I had to come with him. I held out my two arms as if to say, "Go ahead and put me in hand cuffs."

He said, "Put your hands down, dummy, and come with me."

He let me sit in the front seat of his patrol car so we could talk. We sat out in front of my house for a while and just talked about where I had been. He didn't realize I had just returned from Vietnam. He asked me my side of the story. I told him and he said he would have to arrest me. I understood completely. He told my mom I would be out of jail in about an hour, and she could come and pick me up then. She thanked him, and we were off to the police station.

He took me to a little room and took my statement. Another officer I didn't know in civilian clothes came in. The police officer I knew told him what had happened. The guy in civilian clothes told me I was released, but I would have to show up in two days for a hearing. The judge would figure out what he was going to do with me. I was charged with assault and trespassing. The officer told me when I showed up before the judge to wear my uniform with all my ribbons. That would probably win me some points with the judge because he was a World War II veteran.

A few days later, my mother and I went to see the judge. I had a fresh high-and-tight haircut, clean and pressed uniform with all my ribbons on, and I was standing tall, looking good, ought to be in Hollywood. The guy I beat up came in with his father and mother. He looked like hell. He had long, dirty hair, and his clothes looked like he had slept in them. His mouth was all jacked up where I had punched him. His lip was swollen and I noticed for the first time he had braces, so my punches to his mouth had done their job. I almost felt sorry for him—almost. The judge came in not looking at either of us. He stared at my file for a few minutes, then looked up. He only asked me one question. He asked if the Marine Corps had any type of training or briefings on what to expect when we got home from Vietnam with all the protests going on.

I said, "No sir." He then looked back at the file and started writing something. He never looked at or asked the guy I beat up any questions.

He then looked up at me and said, "Young man, I am putting you on notice. If you so much as spit on the sidewalk for the rest of your time on leave, I will have you arrested and returned to military control. You're dismissed."

I was in shock, I thought I was going to jail. The father of the guy I had beaten up had a fit. He couldn't believe the judge let that "animal" go free (referring to me, of course).

I wanted to say something, but my mother grabbed my arm and said, "Lets get out of here."

I just stared at the kid I beat up as if to say, "I'll be seeing you again."

His father continued to rant and rave at the judge as we left. My mother said that I was lucky, and I'd better keep my nose clean the rest of the time I was home. I knew that would be the end of any kind of contact I might have had with my ex-girlfriend. That was okay with me. I had made several friends with other girls since I had been home.

About the same time, my two female cousins from Oklahoma came to town to see me with my aunt, my dad's sister. My cousins were fifteen and sixteen years old. I had another female cousin that lived in Zanesville, also. I decided I was going to take my three female cousins to lunch one day. We were at a restaurant downtown when some guy came up to me and my three cousins and began making rude comments to them. I don't remember this incident. My cousin from Oklahoma reminded me of this while visiting me in 2012. She said I got up and started choking the guy right there in the restaurant. She told me they were scared because they had never seen that side of me before. Several people came over and broke it up before I hurt the guy, they threw him out. I did not remember this incident until she reminded me of it during her visit.

The only other incident I had while on leave was at a Saturday night dance that Ken, Pat, and I went to. I was finally running into a lot of kids I had gone to school with, and it felt good that they actually talked to me. At the dance, I went to the bathroom down a narrow hallway. When I came out, there was the younger brother of the guy I had beaten up. I tried to walk around him, but he wanted a confrontation. My two buddies saw what was going on and waited for the action to start. The kid started mouthing off that his brother was some kind of karate expert and had I not sucker punched him, he would have kicked my ass. I, again, tried to get around him and walk away because of what the judge had said. The kid kept pushing me. Finally, I freaked out on him. I pushed him up against the wall with my forearm in his throat, choking him and cussing him. Again, things became fuzzy. My buddies finally grabbed me and told me we needed to get the hell out of there because someone was calling the police. I let the kid go, and he dropped to the floor trying to catch his breath. We left.

No police officers showed up at my house that night, so I guess nobody really called the police. I do remember hearing yells from the crowd encouraging me to kick his ass, though.

The rest of my time on leave was spent at Swallows trying to pick up girls. I found out it was actually pretty easy. The girls I talked to said they liked me because of how neatly dressed I was and how good I smelled. Good old Brut Cologne.

The day finally came when I had to leave to go back to the Marine Corps. I was excited to get to my next assignment. I was ready to get back to the business of being a Marine. I never did talk to my ex-girlfriend again, but about a month later, I got a letter from my mother telling me my ex-girlfriend had stopped by the house. They had a nice conversation, and Mom said she apologized for hurting me. She brought back all the stuff I had given her over the years, including all the letters I had written her while I was in basic training and Vietnam. She told my mom she guessed it was over between us. *What?* After I got out of the Marine Corps, I burned those letters, plus all the ones she had written me that I had saved all those years.

I settled into my new assignment as a squad leader in Echo Company, Second Battalion, Eighth Marines, Second Marine Division. I found out we would soon be deploying to Guantanamo Bay, Cuba for six months. I wasn't happy with the notion of going overseas again so soon, but it was better than the alternative—going back to Vietnam.

I didn't like being a stateside Marine. Racial tensions were high and everyone seemed to want to grow their hair long. My company deployed to Cuba and stayed there six months guarding the fence line. It wasn't Vietnam, and at least we weren't being shot at.

We would get some action on the fence line occasionally, mostly at night. We would have Cuban defectors climb the fence at night. We weren't allowed to talk to them or touch them. We could only guard them until the sergeant of the guard showed up with a truck to pick them up.

The only scary thing that happened was the Cubans would roll up to the fence line late at night in tanks, turn on the tank's spot lights, point them straight at the bunker we occupied, and rev the engines of the tanks. Our SOP was to get out of the bunker and move to smaller prepared fighting positions on each side of the bunker in case the Cuban's decided to blow up the bunker with the tanks.

There wasn't much to do on our time off. We were allowed to go on three day passes off the island if time permitted. I took advantage of every situation that took me away from the island. I visited Jamaica, Puerto Rico, and Haiti. I was not loving Marine Corps life anymore. I wished I had extended my tour in Vietnam when Bill had extended his.

The six months went by fairly quickly, especially with me being allowed to fly off the island on occasion. I was even promoted to sergeant. I was able to get one hell of a good tan. We were sent back to Camp Lejeune in July just before my twentieth birthday. I really wanted to be at home on leave for my birthday, but it was not to be. I was assigned duties as non-commissioned officer in charge (NCOIC) of a detail that involved moving furniture out of old barracks that were about to be demolished. I hated the duty. I didn't have the original squad I had in Cuba (they had all rotated to new assignments when we returned). I had a bunch of slackers.

With racial tensions being at an all time high, we had to attend classes on how to deal with racial issues. I was hating this more and more each day. I would always say everyone was the same color: green. I never saw race as an issue, especially in Vietnam. Everybody was treated the same, and that's how I managed my details. I treated everyone the same and even helped with the lifting, even though I didn't have to as the NCOIC.

One day, this young black private refused to do any more lifting. I ordered him to work, but he refused. We were standing beside the truck we were loading when he decided he wanted to stick his chest out and challenge me. I cut loose on him. I beat the living crap out of him. I knew after it was over and I dragged him into the first sergeant's office that I had screwed up. The only thing that saved me was the truck driver. He was also a young black kid, but didn't believe in all the black power rhetoric that seemed to be infiltrating Camp Lejeune. He told the first sergeant the private attacked me, and I was only defending myself. The private was charged with assault and was eventually discharged from the Marine Corps, and I was relieved from the detail.

Around the end of July 1969, a bunch of us were called out of formation one morning and told to go to the post theater for a briefing. We had no idea what was going on, but all of us were Vietnam veterans who had less than a year to do until we were to be discharged from the Marine Corps. We were afraid we were going to be told we were going back to "The Nam," as we called it. I just wanted to do my year and go home. I had no intention of staying in the Corps one day longer than I had to.

By the time we got there, about forty or fifty other Marines were also there. A lieutenant came out and started briefing us about what the Marine Corps had to offer. We were in a reenlistment briefing. I had two friends in the theater with me, and we just kind of laughed to ourselves. There was no way the Marines were going to get anything else out of any of us.

A Marine Corps recruiter came out and offered a tour on Recruiting Duty in the city of our choice. They almost had me there. Then a Marine Corps drill instructor came out and talked about being a drill instructor. I hated my DI, so there was no way I could see myself being one of those guys. Several others came out offering $10,000 bonuses and other benefits. They even offered to let us reenlist to go back to Vietnam. That came with a $10,000 tax free bonus, and thirty days free leave. I guess the Marines were having problems keeping people in if they were offering good stuff like that.

After all the briefings were finished, the lieutenant came back out. He said that if any of us wanted to take advantage of what was being offered, to go to the tables in the back and meet with each of the reenlistment NCO's waiting. A lot of guys got up and went to the tables, leaving about ten of us still seated. The lieutenant then gave us some very good news. The Marine Corps would offer those of us remaining an early out. Of course, we ask, "How early?" He said it could be one month or eleven months, depending on how much time we had left and our MOS. I signed up immediately, as did both of my friends. We asked what was going to happen next. He said we would be notified in the next couple of days of our new expiration of term of service (ETS). I was just hoping to be home by Christmas. I didn't want to spend one more Christmas in the Marine Corps.

We went back to the company and reported to the first sergeant. We told him what had happened, and he wasn't happy. He called us several names and told us to get the hell out of his office. He just couldn't understand why we didn't want to be a lifer like him.

A couple of days later, the three of us were called to the first sergeant's office. He didn't have a pleasant look on his face. He said he had received our orders with our new ETS. We were expecting a six to eight month drop. He then announced our new ETS was 8 August 1969. Holy crap! We would be out of the Marine Corps in less than a week, not six or eight months. We all hollered like a bunch of school girls. The first sergeant kicked us out of his office again and told us to report to personnel to out process out of the Marine Corps. It was one of the happiest days of my life.

During the out processing physical examination, something came up that almost ruined my plans for discharge. The Doctor examining me noticed that I had never been medically cleared to return to full duty due to my disease of unknown origin from Vietnam. That damn disease of unknown origin was back to haunt me. He said I could do one of two things. He could send me to Walter Reed Army Hospital in Washington, DC, for a complete examination, which would stop my getting out of the Marine Corps early, or I could sign a waiver, and he would clear me. I signed the waiver.

I didn't call my mom to tell her I was getting out. I decided to give her one more surprise and just show up as a civilian. At least I didn't have a girlfriend to surprise.

Less than a week later, I was out of the Marine Corps and on a bus on my way back to Zanesville, Ohio. I had gotten out just in time to enroll in college. Even though I was not a very good student in high school, I was determined to be a good college student.

My bus arrived in Zanesville early the next morning. I was a civilian. I called a taxi and had him take me home. I didn't know it at the time, but my aunt and two cousins were visiting from California. I walked in the back door of our house to see them all eating breakfast. What a great homecoming. My mother thought something was wrong because I wasn't due home. She was extremely happy to see me and to know I was a civilian again. The only one that was not happy was my idiot stepfather. He thought I should have stayed in the Marine Corps. He just didn't want me in the house anymore. Too bad, I was home for good.

This book ends just like it started. I was sitting on my mom's couch, in our living room, in the exact spot where the recruiter and I were sitting more than two years before. This time I was more mature, wiser to the ways of the world, very angry, and riddled with guilt. It wasn't until some thirty-eight years later that I would learn where all that anger and guilt came from. I was diagnosed with Post Traumatic Stress Disorder in 2006. I could finally put an end to the years of anger, torment, and survival guilt I had felt since 1968. Or could I?

THE END

AFTERWORD

The week after I got out of the Marine Corps, college enrollment started at the Zanesville campus of Ohio University. I went and stood in line with a lot of the kids I had gone to school with. They were all two years behind me in high school, but we would enter college together. I talked to several girls there including twins that would not give me the time of day in high school, but seemed to be all over me. I guess it was my Brut cologne again.

While talking to the counselor about what I wanted to major in, he suggested I major in journalism. He said he thought I might be good at that, so that's what I did. I would become a journalist.

As I was talking to several girls, I noticed a very pretty girl standing looking at me. It was my ex-girlfriend. The girls I was standing in line with saw her too, and asked if I was going to go talk to her. I said no, and just smiled and waived at her. She smiled and waived back.

I didn't much like being around crowds by then, and my paranoia was running deep. I could just feel people staring at me and I didn't like it. It was probably all my imagination, but I didn't know that at the time.

My GI bill did not come through before school started, so I didn't go. My mother offered to pay for my tuition, and said I could pay her back when my GI bill came through, but I declined. I didn't like to idea of borrowing money from my mom with my stepfather watching my every move. I guess I wouldn't become a journalist.

I got a job, and the next few months were filled with drunken nights and lots of fights. I bought myself a 1949 Plymouth to drive around in. I loved that old car. It was impossible to tear up, and believe me I tried.

Finally, I met the woman I would marry. We met on a visit downtown one day. I was trying to date this girl I had known for a long time, but she wasn't interested. She introduced me to the girl that would become my wife. We dated for about a year before getting married.

We are still married to this day. We have two great kids and four wonderful grandchildren. My days and nights of drunken brawls were over. We were married for almost two years and my wife was pregnant for our second child when the factory I was working for went on strike. I couldn't afford a second child with no insurance and no job; I had to look for an alternative. I really missed the military life, so I went and saw a Marine recruiter. I told him my situation. He said I could go back into the Marine Corps, but I would have to go back as a lance corporal and go back to basic training. There was no way I would do Marine Corps basic training again, so I thanked him and left. I then went to an Army recruiter, who offered me corporal and waived basic training. I would have to go in as a grunt, but that was okay with me.

My wife had no idea what I had done. I hadn't talked to her about it. I just showed up at home that afternoon with a high and tight haircut. She just stared at me and asked me what I had done. I told her, and she was in shock. After the shock wore off, we talked, and I told her why I'd done it. I would be heading off in two weeks to Fort Knox, Kentucky, for issue of my Army equipment and uniforms, then I'd be assigned somewhere else in the world. Vietnam was still a real possibility. In the back of my mind, I was hoping to go back to Vietnam. I think the guilt of surviving it the first time, while many good friends of mine had not, weighed heavy on my mind. I had business to finish over there.

Two weeks later, I reported to Fort Knox. After about three weeks of processing, I got my first assignment in the Army. I was to be a squad leader in Charlie Company, First Battalion, Sixtieth Infantry Regiment, 172d Artic Light Infantry Brigade, Fort Richardson, Alaska. What a shock, Alaska. I didn't even know there were troops in Alaska, let alone an Infantry unit.

My Army career had started off in Alaska. I thrived in the Army. To tell the truth, I was a much better soldier than I was ever a Marine. I excelled in the Army. I was always promoted ahead of my peers. I even completed two and a half years as a, you guessed it, drill instructor, except in the Army they're called drill sergeants. I loved the Army and spent the next twenty-eight years traveling the world. I had many varying assignments culminating as the senior enlisted advisor to the North Carolina National Guard, an assignment that I hated.

I finally retired as a Sergeant Major in 1998. I loved the military and will say to this day that the military, and my wife, saved my life. I was a bad civilian. I was destined to be in the military I guess.

I did find out while at my fifteen year class reunion that my ex-girlfriend and her hippy boyfriend had gotten married. I found out also, they had gotten divorced. I guess what goes around comes around. I didn't have any feelings about it one way or the other. Well, maybe I did. I guess the whole revenge thing came back into play for me.

I now live the happy retired life in north Georgia. I love it here. My family lives around me, and after much encouragement from family and friends, got the gumption to write my story. Maybe I did finally become a journalist after all.

APPENDIX A

FRANK POWERS
BRONZE STAR CITATION

For heroic achievement in connection with operations against insurgent communist (Viet Cong) forces in the Republic of Vietnam while serving as a Squad Leader with Company K, Third Battalion, Seventh Marines, First Marine Division. On the morning of 16 February, 1968, Corporal Powers' squad was providing security for an engineer unit which was conducting a search for mines and other explosive devices along a road near Da Nang. Suddenly, the unit was ambushed by a large Viet Cong force. Reacting instantly, Corporal Powers unhesitatingly exposed himself to the hostile fire in order to deploy his squad. Fearlessly moving from one position to another, he skillfully directed fire of his men and then ran to a nearby tank to pinpoint the enemy positions for the vehicle's gunner. Returning to his squad, Corporal Powers radioed for supporting arms fire and, when informed that his squad had sustained casualties, again exposed himself to the enemy fire while moving to assist the wounded Marines. Ignoring the hostile fire, Corporal Powers skillfully assisted the casualties and ably rendered medical assistance to the units corpsman when he was subsequently wounded. His professionalism and sincere concern for the welfare of his comrades inspired all who observed him and were instrumental in forcing the enemy to break contact. Corporal Powers' courage, bold initiative and steadfast devotion to duty in the face of great personal danger were in keeping with the highest traditions of the Marine Corps and of the United States Naval Service.

Corporal Powers is authorized to wear the Combat "V"
Signed for the President

V. H. Krulak
Lieutenant General, U. S. Marine Corps
Commanding General
Fleet Marine Force, Pacific

APPENDIX B

WAYNE CARON'S
MEDAL OF HONOR CITATION

For conspicuous gallantry and intrepidity at the risk of his life above and beyond the call of duty on 28 July, 1968 while serving as a Platoon Corpsman with Company K, Third Battalion, Seventh Marines, First Marine Division during combat operations against enemy forces in the Republic of Vietnam. While on a sweep through an open rice field in Quang Nam Province, Petty Officer Caron's unit started receiving enemy small-arms fire. Upon seeing two Marine casualties fall, he immediately ran forward to render first aid, but found that they were dead. At this time, the platoon was taken under intense small-arms fire and automatic weapons fire, sustaining additional casualties. As he moved to the aid of his wounded comrades, Petty Officer Caron was hit in the arm by enemy fire. Although knocked to the ground, he regained his feet and continued to the injured Marines. He rendered medical assistance to the first Marine he reached, who was grievously wounded, and undoubtedly was instrumental in saving a man's life. Petty Officer Caron then ran toward the second wounded Marine, but was again hit by enemy fire, this time in the leg. Nonetheless, he crawled the remaining distance and provided medical assitance for this severely wounded man. Petty Officer Caron continued to make his way to yet another injured comrade, when he was again struck by enemy small-arms fire. Courageously and with unbelievable determination, Petty Officer Caron continued his attempt to reach the third Marine until he was killed by an enemy rocket round. His inspiring valor, steadfast determination, and selfless dedication to duty in the face of extreme danger, sustain and enhance the finest traditions of the United States Navel Service. He gallantly gave his life in the service of his country.

Richard M. Nixon

APPENDIX C

LIST OF MARINES KILLED IN ACTION FROM KILO THIRD AND SEVENTH

Lest We Forget

Forever on the Wall

1965

PFC Thomas Robert Ames, 29 June
PFC Gordon James Deitz Jr., 4 July
LCPL Alvin Chester, 5 July
LCPL Adolpho A Taboada Jr., 24 October

1966

PFC Allan Michael Tanguay, 10 March
LCPL Harold Wendell Wilson, 21 March
HM3 William Ervin Burke III, 22 March
PFC Bruce Randolph Landis Jr., 22 March
LCPL Richard Anthony Caruolo, 23 March
PFC Richard Francis Babala, 11 April
LCPL Gerald William Engel, 18 April
LCPL Michael George Barton, 13 July
PFC Robert D Weaver, 24 October
PFC Donald R Brunner, 4 November
PFC Philip A Purvis, 25 November

1967

LCPL Edward C McCarthy, 2 February
PVT Larry B Wynne, 19 February
PVT Joseph Leonard, 5 March
LCPL Robert Lee Spires, 5 March
LCPL Steven Gary Bloom, 8 March
SGT Angel Mendez, 16 March
SGT Woodrow C Hurlock, 27 March
LCPL Francis M Lawrence Jr., 2 April
LCPL David Bruce Koenig, 3 May
PFC Gerald Alan Champion, 31 May
CPL Russell Rene Roulier, 21 June
SGT Bing Forest Stephans, 29 June
LCPL Walter Wayne Vinson, 30 June
LCPL Frederick Albert Newby Jr., 6 August
LCPL Roy Mitchel Wheat, 11 August
LCPL David Lee McMath, 12 August
LCPL Lucion Gillispie Jr., 21 August
LCPL Charles Paul Sircher, 18 September
PFC Raymond Patrick Finley, 1 October
2LT John Alexander Norris III, 4 October
PVT Luther Elmer Preston, 5 November
CPL Richard Maxwell Hoots, 9 November
CPL Timothy Morgan Dick, 11 December
LCPL Verne Lyle Johnson Jr., 13 December
LCPL Dennis Leon Senz, 18 December
PFC Larry Eugene Gonzalez, 21 December
CPL James McMurry McClean, 21 December

1968

PFC Donald Bryan Olsen, 12 February
PFC Gregory William Fischer, 22 February
PFC Michael Lane Charles, 3 March
PFC George Larry Starks, 18 March
PFC Michael D Lawrence, 23 March
PFC Danny Eugene Tucker, 23 March
LCPL MARVIN EARL GALBRAITH, 27 March
LCPL Richard Lopez, 27 March
PFC Sherrick Camden Britton, 10 April
PFC John Stephen Westphal, 13 April
LCPL Steve Davis, 24 April
LCPL Frank Rudolph Simmons, 24 April
PFC Donald Ray Hayes, 6 May
CPL Daryl La Don Stith, 20 May
PFC James Lee Luttrell, 21 June
PFC John Fonseca, 26 June
PVT James Weldon Davis, 4 July
CPL John Butler Murray, 5 July
PVT Roscoe David Adams, 28 July
SSGT David Leroy Brooks, 28 July
HM3 Wayne Maurice Caron, 28 July
PFC George Lee Carr, 28 July
CPL Edward Joseph Downs, 28 July
CPL Philip Lyn Gosselin, 28 July
PFC Ray Glenwood Hawk, 28 July
LCPL George Stephen Johnson, 28 July
LCPL Douglas Milton Kelly, 28 July
PFC John Manning Lancaster, 28 July
LCPL Robert Charles Lee, 28 July
CPL Daniel Edward Lloyd, 28 July

LCPL James Calvin Markel, Jr 28 July
LCPL Carl Robert Miller, 28 July
CPL Anthony Carlos Pino, 28 July
LCPL Raphael Johnny Rendon, 28 July
PVT John Edward Rice, 28 July
CPL John Reyito Serrano, 28 July
2LT William Stanley Smoyer, 28 July
PVT John Jeremiah Till, 28 July
LCPL Richard Edward Urban, 28 July
PFC Michael Allen Griggs, 2 August
PFC Peter John Lovan, 2 August
CPL Tom Dennis Sugiura, 2 September
CPL Marlen Le Roy Phillips, 6 September
PFC William James Pinter, 12 September
CPL Phillip Felix Kaplon Jr., 7 November
CPL Claud William Capraro, 3 December
LCPL John Francis Kanaczet Jr., 5 December
2LT James Monroe Rushing, 16 December
PFC Jerry Don Gibbs, 30 December
PFC Roger Dale Sprinkle, 30 December
PFC John Jacob McLay Jr., 31 December

1969

PFC Frankie Ross Williams, 4 February
LCPL Charles Nick Bondi, 14 February
SGT Alfredo Julian Villanueva, 20 February
LCPL Timothy Lawrence Gilson, 23 February
HN Larry Anthony Hartigan, 23 February
LCPL William Reuben Hodge, 23 February
PFC Robert Albert Horcajo, 23 February
LCPL Jesse Manuel Nunez, 23 February

PFC Salvador Lopez Norzagaaray, 26 February
HM3 Lewis Craig Harris, 11 March
PFC Roger Wayne Cummings, 20 April
PFC Bernard George Oliver Jr., 21 April
LCPL Bernard Fredrick Ritchie, 21 April
LCPL Charles Jackson Wilson, 21 April
PFC Larry Keith Henson, 8 May
PFC Charles Edgar Outman, 8 May
PFC Charles Jeffrey Freeland, 10 May
PFC Henry Garcia Jr., 10 May
PFC Patrick Edward Murphy, 10 May
PFC Brent Thomas Mascher, 13 May
PFC Graham Hughes, 23 May
CPL Frederick Lee Benishek, 7 June
LCPL Raymond Clark Holman, 16 June
CPL Harvey Albert Duhy Jr., 19 June
PFC Bruce Edwin Ingman, 14 July
Johnny Steve Bosser, 28 August
CPL Charles C Buchanan, 28 August
PFC Dennis Dean Davis, 28 August
LCPL Jose Francisco Jimenez, 28 August
LCPL Robert Warren McCabe, 28 August
Clarence H Saint Clair Jr., 28 August
PFC Edward Herbert Sherrod, 28 August
PFC David N Hebert, 25 October
LCPL Michael John Rodowicz, 25 October
PFC William Calvin James, 19 November
PFC Alfred Lacy Williams, 23 December

1970

PFC Keith Bernell Lackey, 16 January
PFC Arthur William Kinser, 14 February
SGT John L Pena, 24 April
CPL Roy L Wilson, 11 May
LCPL Jose C Montano, 8 August
PVT James M Doty, 31 July
PFC James Kevin Musselman, 31 July
LCPL Phillip A Paule, 31 July
PFC Gregg A Smith, 31 July
SGT David W Baker, 18 September

RIP